EVERYDAY
WISDOM

Book Design by Paul Ferrini
and Lisa Carta

Cover art: Sybil by Dosso Dossi
Back cover: St Matthew from the Gospel Book of Charlemagne

Library of Congress Control Number: 20022106489

ISBN 1-879159-51-1

Manufactured in the United States of America

Heartways Press
P.O. Box 99, Greenfield MA 01302

Manufactured in the United States of America

EVERYDAY WISDOM

PAUL FERRINI

iNtROÒUctioN

everyday Wisdom contains a spiritual reading for each day of the year. The readings that comprise this book have been adapted from the *Weekly Wisdom Message* and *Ask Paul* sections of my website (www.paulferrini.com) where I answer questions from readers on a variety of topics such as relationships, addiction, career, money, sex, child-rearing, dealing with anger and guilt and so on.

My answers offer no shortcuts or quick fixes. Instead, they place the responsibility for meaningful change on the shoulders of the questioners and challenge them to look more deeply at their experience. This book asks the same of you.

While I hope these readings will uplift and inspire you, their primary purpose is to help you look within yourself for the answers. For within every question is the seed of an answer. This book is just a compass pointing you in the direction where the answer lies. When you start moving in that direction, you get on track with your own intuitive wisdom. And that is the true guide that will lead you to clarity and to peace.

This book can be used as a Spiritual Book of Days or as a Spiritual Oracle. To use it as a Book of Days, just read the narrative associated with the day in question. To use it as a Spiritual Oracle, just purchase the companion deck of Wisdom Cards (sold separately) and follow the instructions that come with it.

You can use this book a source for daily inspiration, referring to the daily message as a subject for reflection when you wake up in the morning or go to bed at night. If you use it in this way, it is often helpful to combine it with a daily practice of journaling. On some days, the message may seem especially poignant and relevant to your life. On other days it may not. Yet, if you pay attention during the day, you may find that you notice events, behaviors or conversations that evoke the message for that day. Make note of these examples, as they will help you to understand and integrate the spiritual principles expressed in this book into your daily life.

A SPIRITUAL ORACLE

The other way to use *Everyday Wisdom* is in conjunction with the companion deck of *Wisdom Cards*. These cards feature beautiful Renaissance paintings evoking archetypal themes. Each card is associated with one of the lunar months in this book. The *Wisdom Cards* come with a detailed instruction booklet describing a divinatory procedure that will direct you to a specific reading in this book in answer to your question. The *Wisdom Cards* can also be used to pinpoint the best timeframes for an action or event.

I hope that the readings in this book will bring you into a deeper relationship to yourself. May you learn to ask the right questions and open yourself to the Source of Wisdom within your own consciousness. May these words point you to the place of silent knowing within which is beyond words. May they help you find patience, acceptance and compassion for yourself and others. *Namaste,*

A Spiritual Book of Days

december 22

The Holy Grail

We go all over the world looking for love, searching in this place or that place, in this person or in that person. We look everywhere for it except within our own hearts and minds.

When you realize that you are the Source of this ever-elusive love you are seeking, you have the most important piece of knowledge available to you. It will save you many useless journeys. It will keep you from going down thousands of roads that lead only to cul de sacs, aborted promises and shortcuts that never materialize

december 23

A Fire Alarm

When you have pain in your life you automatically tense up. You resist the pain or you fight it. Unfortunately, that just makes the pain hang around.

Through experience you learn that the way out of pain is not to resist it but to accept it. One way you can begin to accept it is to see the pain not as an attack on you or as a punishment of you, but as a communication that tells you something is awry. It is like a fire alarm that wakes you up before the fire engulfs you. It is a messenger telling you that you need to adjust something in your life that is out of balance.

december 24

Mutual Respect

a ny meaningful consensus comes out of the atmosphere of mutual respect.

We find equality with others by recognizing that there are many ways of looking at any situation and we have only one of them. Listening to others, respecting their ideas and experiences, helps to open us to a wider spectrum of reality. It enables us to open up the doors of our conceptual prison and see things from a new perspective.

december 25

Opening to Love

e very lesson that comes into your life asks you to open your heart and mind in a new way. Old defense mechanisms that are no longer needed for your survival must be surrendered. Inch by inch, the territory claimed by fear must open to love's embrace.

december 26

Listening for Truth

You are responsible for what you believe, even if you choose to believe what others tell you. So don't be afraid to question the authority of others. No one knows better than you do what you truly need.

However, you will not align with truth if you remain focused in your ego structure. You need to go much deeper than that. You need to find that which supports you in expressing yourself without hurting others. And you also need to find that which supports others in expressing themselves without hurting you.

december 27

The Play of Shadows

Everything you are afraid of is personified somehow. Yet it belongs to you. The people who push your buttons are personifications of your own shadow. Often, you return the favor, pushing their buttons too. Then, your relationship becomes the relationship of one shadow to another.

Only when you wake up and understand that the interaction is about your own shadow—what you hate, cannot accept or fear about yourself—are you able to unhook emotionally, because only then will you stop projecting your fears onto others.

december 28

The Lesson of Abuse

If you want to understand the cycle of violence, begin by understanding your part in it. Do you identify with the victim or the abuser, or both?

Keep in mind that victimizers have usually been victims in the past. That is how the cycle of violence continues. It is passed down through the generations until someone sees the whole pattern and decides to change it in him or herself.

Are you that person? Are you willing to look at yourself that deeply?

Victims need to understand how to stand up for themselves without attacking others. Victimizers have the same lesson.

december 29

A Perfect Boomerang

Whether you know it or not, the only person you can attack is yourself. You may believe that you are attacking someone else, but that's just an illusion.

Everything that you attempt to project onto others comes home to you. Thought is a perfect boomerang. It always returns to the person who sent it.

december 30

Surrendering Judgment

One of the most important spiritual practices is to let things be as they are without interpretation, without embellishment, without judgment. That immediately gives the ego a coronary. Imagine telling the ego it cannot judge, compare, interpret? What then is it going to do? It doesn't really know how to do anything else.

Of course, as soon as we try to tell the ego not to judge, a whole new layer of judgment comes up. The layers are endless. But that's why the process is so rich.

december 31

Perceptions

Learning the lessons life brings takes a great deal of patience and compassion. We need to realize that it isn't easy for us to change how we perceive reality. If it was, we wouldn't need so many lessons.

Most of our lessons do not ask us to change ourselves, others or the world. They ask us to change our perception of ourselves, other people, and the world around us.

january 1

Authenticity

on't be concerned that your path is not like that of others. It takes courage to be yourself and not to live in reaction to the likes and dislikes of others. Be courageous and follow your heart. You need to walk your own unique path in order to honor yourself and fulfill your spiritual purpose.

If your life direction makes other people uncomfortable, then they do not have to share the journey with you. Don't be disappointed, if this is the case. When others choose to leave, it is usually because they must move in a different direction to honor themselves.

january 2

Changing an Old Pattern

t doesn't work when you take responsibility for how others feel or make others responsible for how you feel. It doesn't work when you ask others to fix things for you or when you try to fix things for others. These old patterns need to be changed. They do not empower you, nor do they empower others. You can create a new pattern by letting others off the hook and taking responsibility for your life right now.

january 3

Misperception

as long as you do not perceive reality accurately you will attract a correction to that misperception. Often you interpret the correction as an attack. It isn't. It is an opportunity for you to see the distortion that fear has created in your thinking and to correct your vision so that you can see what is really there.

january 4

Standing up for Yourself without Attacking Others

if you are triggered by someone, acknowledge your reactivity. Don't react and attack. Don't blame. Don't project.

Don't try to make someone else responsible for what you are thinking or feeling. Own your thoughts and feelings totally. And then communicate them to those who need to understand.

Say "This is about me, not about you. This is what is happening for me right now." That is how the cycle of violence is broken.

january 5

Asking for Love

When you make friends with the child within, s/he ceases to be afraid to ask for the love that s/he wants and needs. Instead of trying to manipulate and control to get some substitute for love, s/he just asks for love directly.

When the child knows that she is loved in the midst of her hurt and sadness, her discomfort begins to fade. Her sense of separation begins to be bridged.

Something happens when we know that we are loved, but it can't happen until we know that love is what we want and we have the courage to ask for it.

january 6

Self-Forgiveness

The process of forgiveness starts in your own heart. It has very little to do with others.

It is easy to forgive others when you have already forgiven yourself. But it's impossible to forgive others if you have not forgiven yourself.

january 7

Forgiveness is a Process

forgiveness does not happen all at once. It is a process that may take weeks, even months or years. The important thing is to remember that each gesture of forgiveness is sufficient. Whatever we can do now is enough. The rest will happen when we are ready.

If we want to be genuine in our process, we need to do what we can now and forgive ourselves for all the ways in which we are still unwilling or unable to forgive.

january 8

The Light of the World

You are the light of the world, but you do not know it because you have not looked deeply enough into your own heart. Take a moment to look. Take a moment to find the light that dances in the dark night within. See those deep colors penetrating the black clouds, the hands of light reaching to the horizon. Until you can see the light in yourself you cannot bring it to the world.

january 9

Ecstasy

every moment is ecstatic if we take the time to experience it fully. So keep your eyes and your heart open, welcome each moment as it comes, and bless it as it goes. Know that everything is okay just the way it is. Every experience you have had has already been forgiven. You are not a prisoner the past. You are free to respond with love and truth in this moment.

january 10

Communication is a Sacred Act

Listening takes energy and attention. It takes receptivity to the other person. When we aren't receptive, we should not try to listen. We should let the other person know that we are not in a receptive state. Conversely, when the other person cannot offer this attention to us, we shouldn't try to share with him or her.

Communication does not happen by itself. It requires both the speaker and the listener to be present. When both are present fully, it is a sacred act.

january 11

Cults vs Ministries

Groups that create spiritual hierarchies, restrict the physical or intellectual freedom of their members, or exclude others from their acceptance and love are cults.

Jesus was a great teacher because he didn't exclude anyone. He saw no difference between your soul and the soul of the addict or prostitute. He ministered to the lepers and the untouchables just as he ministers to you and to me.

Only one who ever so deeply knows that S/he is God can see God in everyone. And those who don't know it that deeply should hold their tongues.

january 12

Acting for the Good of All

There is at all times and under all circumstances a course of action that honors all of the people involved, but it cannot be found until the thoughts and feelings of all people have been honored.

january 13

The Dance and the Destination

i n the end, all lakes and rivers empty into the sea. All forms of love merge into divine, unconditional love, the essence of who and what we are.

All of us are pulled by an inner current to be born, to grow, to individuate and to merge into the greater whole. That is the divine dance.

The beauty is that all this happens by itself. We do not have to do anything to make it happen.

january 14

A Feast is Born

W hen one person brings a fish and another brings a loaf of bread, a feast is born. There always seems to be more than enough food to go around when everyone brings something.

When your gift is offered with no strings attached, it multiplies. One fish becomes two, and two become four. Your gift feeds others and their gift feeds you.

When we think of the story of the loaves and the fishes, we think of it as a solo performance. But Jesus was showing each of us what to do. He was inviting us to a harvest of an empowered community, where each person's gift is authentic and an essential part of the meal of life.

january 15

Prosperity

many people want to be helpers, but they do not help themselves. They feed others, but they do not feed themselves. Is it any wonder that they burn out, become tired and disillusioned?

If you are not fed by what you do, how can you feed others? Your happiness is not secondary. It is of primary importance. Abundance flows from your happiness. The gifts of God flow through your love and acceptance of yourself.

When you are honest, you see that the aspects of your life that prosper are the ones that bring you the most joy. They are areas to which you give your greatest energy and attention.

january 16

Sacrifice

there is always more of a good thing. If love feels good to you there will be more of it. If money feels good to you, you will attract more money. If what you do with your time feels good, you will have more time to do it.

But if you do not enjoy these things, you will have less of them. What you do not enjoy does not prosper. What you do out of sacrifice or guilt becomes difficult, problematic.

You can do a million affirmations and it won't make any difference. The universe does not support what you do out of sacrifice or guilt. It's that simple.

january 17

Inappropriate Responsibility

You are not responsible for the thoughts, feelings or actions of other people, even if you are involved in their lives. When others try to blame you or make you responsible for what has happened to them, they are not acting in good faith.

Your responsibility is to accept and honor what others are experiencing, but not to take responsibility for it. Their experience belongs to them. They are responsible for what they think, what they say and what they do.

january 18

Empowerment Without Spiritual Pride

You must empower and believe in yourself. If you are afraid to take risks for fear of failing or losing the approval of others, you won't accomplish very much in life.

You must have the courage to be yourself fully, but you also must guard against overconfidence and insensitivity toward others. Power without humility will not serve you. Spiritual pride is as big an impediment on the path as is victim consciousness.

january 19

Appropriate Responsibility

You are responsible for making your own choices and for learning from the mistakes that you make. It is not appropriate for you to make decisions for others or to let them make decisions for you.

january 20

Inner Perfection

Each person is whole and complete even though he may not believe it himself, even though others may see him as deficient. If you would see a person through the eyes of Spirit, you must look past his apparent weaknesses and see his inner perfection. Even if he attacks you, you must realize that he just wants your love and attention and does not know how to ask for it.

jaNuaRy 21

Seeing with Love

the world will never be good unless you are willing to see its goodness. What you experience depends on how you look at things. When you look with judgment, life is twisted and empty. When you look with an open heart and mind, life is poignant and meaningful.

Whatever you see without love you separate from. You do this to try to alleviate your fear. But the more you separate, the less connection you feel with others and the more fearful you become.

The only thing that can successfully address your fear is to hold it with love. As soon as you look with love, you see a different world.

jaNuaRy 22

Your Affirming Presence

your suffering results from your refusal to accept and bless your life just the way it is now, from your persistent need to try to fix yourself, your relationships and the world you live in. When you stop finding fault with your life, you inhabit it more fully and then it has energy, purpose and integrity.

The only reason your life seems to lack these ingredients now is that your affirming presence is missing. When you are present, there is nothing broken or lacking in your life. It is perfect just as it is.

january 23

Realizing Your Perfection

Perfection is never about the past or the future. It is always and only about now. You are perfect right now regardless of what you are thinking and feeling, regardless of your perceived problems or unfinished business. You are perfect no matter how many mistakes you think you have made. There is nothing you have thought, felt or done that prevents you from realizing your perfection right here and right now.

january 24

Life is Our Teacher

Life is our teacher and we can learn from whatever it brings us. Of course, we don't always like what shows up.

When life asks us to go deeper in our understanding and compassion, we don't always want to do it. We are satisfied with the level that we have.

We can protest our marching orders when we get them, but that won't stop us from marching. We don't get to say "no" to our life.

The healing and redemptive power of experience lies in its ability to help us access and give birth to the deepest part of ourselves. That is why spiritual challenges are a necessary part of our growth.

january 25

Freedom

Being free has nothing to do with leaving the body or the earth. Being free means letting go of what isn't true.

january 26

Pessimism about the World

Our pessimism about the world stems from our indictment of ourselves. If we have not learned to hold our fear compassionately and look without judgment on the shadowy aspects of ourselves, we cannot look at the world with acceptance or compassion.

Yet when we embrace our own darkness and find the light within, we begin to see that light in others, even when they present the shadowy aspects of themselves to us. We are no longer intimidated by a world in which violence seems to prevail, for we understand that this is but a symptom of the separated self. It is a heart-rending cry for love, not dissimilar from the one we heard issue from our own lips when we were feeling the pain of separation.

When we have learned to love ourselves in the midst of our pain, we can answer the call for love when it comes to us. Instead of despairing about the violence in the world, we bring love to the people around us who need it most.

january 27

Healing the Divided Self

Our challenge is to learn to accept all of ourselves, not just the parts that we like. Holding all aspects of ourselves gently and with compassion is what heals the divided self and brings unity to our consciousness.

This inner unity represents the birth of the One Self within our consciousness. When the One Self is born within, we no longer see an outward separation between self and other, for each self is the One Self. Every man or woman is either a waking or sleeping Christ or Buddha. One Eternal Self dwells within the heart of all beings.

january 28

Great Spiritual Beings Don't Belong to the Past

Christ, Buddha, Krishna, Lao Tzu and other great spiritual teachers do not belong to the past. If we resonate with their teachings, then they live with us today, in our hearts and minds and in the holy places where we meet.

january 29

Spiritual Unity

here is but one truth, yet each person, each religion and each culture comes to it uniquely. Diversity is our gift to God. It is the divine expressing in many different forms. When we are no longer afraid of our differences, they will cease to divide us.

Unity is God's gift to us. When we remember this gift, we don't get lost in our differences. We don't separate from each other. We don't forget that each path—however different it seems—leads to the same Garden.

Jews don't go to Jewish heaven. Muslims don't go to Muslim heaven. Buddhists, Hindus, Christians don't go to different heavens. Heaven is a place of peace within our hearts and minds where our differences are gracefully accepted and have no power to divide us.

january 30

A Gentle Reminder

our life is not better or worse than someone else's. Every person's life has highs and lows, good and bad, laughter and tears. You don't have to push away the experiences that come to you. There is nothing there unworthy of you. Indeed, if you look without bias, you will see that there is no lesson that comes without a gentle reminder that you are loved and valued exactly as you are.

JANUARY 31

Illuminating the Darkness

I t doesn't work to try to make the dual world singular by denying either darkness or light. Both are present in the world. Both are present in consciousness. If we accept only the light and deny or repress the darkness, we may find that the darkness erupts from our psyches in ways that are quite unexpected and destructive.

The best use of the light is to illuminate the darkness, not to try to make the darkness go away. Illumination brings awareness, understanding, acceptance and ultimately transformation. Even a small light makes the darkness much less scary.

When we view the darkness as "bad" and try to avoid it or repress it, we give it power. Whatever we are afraid of begins to run our life, even if we pretend that we are not afraid.

When we acknowledge that both gods and devils, heaven and hell, light and darkness, commingle within us, we are being honest and authentic. We don't moralize or engage in other forms of spiritual pretense while we carry dark secrets locked away in some back closet.

feBRuaRy 1

Authentic Spirituality

authentic spirituality is not dualistic or one dimensional. It completely embraces our lives.

If you have to deny any aspect of who you are to be spiritual, then you are creating an inauthentic spirituality. True spirituality should be an instrument of revelation, not a tool for denial.

How can you dwell with God if you refuse to be honest about who you are? God doesn't ask you to pretend to be someone or something you are not. God wants you to be who you are with all your contradictions and dichotomies.

Truth may be difficult, but it has its own durable beauty. Lies might appear beautiful on the surface, but if you look beneath the surface, you won't like what you see.

feBRuaRy 2

Resistance

esires can be a big smoke screen. You think that you need someone or something, but it isn't true. Only when you resist what is here do you desire what is not.

february 3

Teaching Truth

The Ten Commandments are fairly simple and straightforward, yet we have a hard time keeping them. And what do we do with people who break the commandments: excommunicate them, put out their eyes, feed them to the lions?

If you truly believe "Thou shalt not kill," how can you kill the killer? Authentic spiritual teaching proposes to address violence and trespass in a different manner. It suggests that we model the behavior we are expecting from the other person.

If the other person is fearful and strikes out at us and we respond in fear, we have validated his behavior by repeating it. But if we respond to his fear with love, we have stood for the truth and offered him an alternative.

We cannot teach truth by committing error. Only by acting in a truthful manner can we teach what truth is.

february 4

Correction

You do not need to punish yourself or feel guilty about what you have done. Simply acknowledge the truth you have tried to hide from yourself and others. As soon as you recognize your mistake, you have begun to correct it.

february 5

Are our Wounds Real?

The Self is our Spiritual Identity. It is unassailable. It cannot be wounded or broken.

Each Self is equal to every other Self. Inequality is not possible in this dimension of experience. One Self cannot be better than or worse than another.

The drama of abuse happens on the ego level of consciousness, for it is on that level that we believe that one person can be better than another. On that level, there is attack and defense, wounding and healing.

Wounding and healing may have value in a process involving growth in consciousness, but they do not have existential value. One is not worthy or unworthy because one has been wounded. Nor is one worthy or unworthy because one has healed or has not healed from the wound.

The wound is a teaching about forgiveness, both to the one who gave the wound and the one who received it. Once they have offered forgiveness to themselves and to each other, the wound no longer has any meaning.

february 6

The Origin of Conflict

Only because we believe that we are separate do our needs seem to conflict. Of course, our separation is not ultimately real. Separation happens when fear comes up. It is a temporary phenomenon. When we take it seriously we merely enshrine and institutionalize our fear.

february 7

A Positive Outcome

Only your fear causes you to forget that a positive outcome can be realized in any situation.

By being aware of your fear, you minimize its power to color or distort the meaning of the situation before you.

february 8

Compassion

It's easy to love the people who are kind to you, but not so easy to love the people who dislike you or attack you. True compassion arises when your ability to love no longer depends on how others treat you.

february 9

Things Fall Apart

Sometimes life comes in waves and each wave is a purification, a dissolution of attachments, a wiping clean of the slate of judgment and evaluation.

Old boundaries, old roles, old beliefs and values, old images of self are altered or erased, and a new territory is mapped. The things that used to be priorities for us cease to be so important.

Everything appears to be different now. But something is not different. Something deep inside of us remains the same. Indeed, it comes into sharp focus now.

When the circumference of the circle changes, the core Self asserts itself. That is where we must go to re-center and find direction. That is where we find the foundation on which we can rebuild our lives.

february 10

Equality

If there is one person who is not worthy of your acceptance and love, then you cannot have real equality. If you want equality, do not exclude anyone from your idea of truth or justice.

february 11

The Opportunity to Trust

Sometimes forces far greater than any you can muster assert themselves in your life. Resisting them only makes matters worse. Your only choice is to let go and let things be as they are. Remember, any situation beyond your control offers you the opportunity to love and to trust.

february 12

Criticism

Criticism may not seem like a major trespass, except that it tends to be chronic. Are many small, carefully disguised attacks less hurtful than a single act of hatred or betrayal?

When you see the destructive nature of all criticism, your decision to refrain from criticizing becomes an exercise in non-violence.

february 13

Expressing Love

Love expresses not just when you are speaking and acting in a caring way; it also expresses when you refrain from speaking or acting in an uncaring way. Love reveals itself not only when you bless, but when you decide not to take offense.

feBRuaRy 14

Jealousy and Trust

J ealousy says as much about your trust in yourself as it does about your trust in another. It says just as much about your capacity to betray as it does about someone else's.

If you feel jealous of your partner, don't just focus on your partner's behavior. Ask yourself "Is betrayal an issue that keeps coming up for me?"

If you have a pattern of attracting people who betray you, it may be that betrayal is your issue as well as theirs. If you trusted yourself more, you might have chosen more trustworthy partners. If you had no doubt about your ability to be faithful to others, you might not be so quick to question their fidelity to you.

When you know that you cannot betray yourself or another, you don't generally worry about someone else betraying you. Feelings of jealousy arise not just so that you can question others, but so that you can find the root cause of insecurity in yourself.

feBRuaRy 15

The Future

D on't ask "What blessing will tomorrow bring?" Ask "What blessing can I discover right now?"

You don't need to think about tomorrow when you know that your needs are being met right now.

feBRuaRy 16

Abundance of God

Boundaries cannot contain the formless. The limited mind cannot contain the mind of God.

God is without limits, without boundaries. No matter how much wine we pour into the cup, it never gets filled up. There is no limit to the amount of love we can give or receive.

You see the abundance of God is not to be found in some future time. It is here right now.

feBRuaRy 17

False Identity

Your spiritual growth does not happen when you are peaceful and content. It happens when you get angry, sad, greedy, jealous, critical, impatient. It happens when you lose your "spiritual mask," and realize that you are not superman or woman, but just an ordinary human being learning how to love.

february 18

Self Crucifixion

You think that you are pushing against others in order to protect yourself, but it is not true. While you self-righteously charge out in full cinematic color onto the great three dimensional battlefield, a little boy or girl is being crucified in black and white in some lonely cubbyhole of the soul.

Unfortunately, the great battlefield is an illusion. The more you push, the more pressure you put on yourself.

february 19

Surrender

Surrender means that you stop taking issue with life. You realize that you don't have to like or dislike what happens. You just need to accept it.

As you work with surrendering you encounter your resistance. You see how you hold onto things or run away from them. You feel injured, abandoned, anxious or disappointed by what happens. You feel victimized or angry.

Every time you surrender ego, more ego comes up. That is the nature of the process. It doesn't mean that you are doing anything incorrectly. It just means that you are going deeper.

february 20

An Empty Mirror

What is in the mind does not belong to the mind. The content of consciousness flows in and out. But mind is not the content.

Attachment to content, or resistance to it, creates a log-jam in the river of mind. It complicates and confuses. It is an attempt to control what cannot be controlled.

Just watch your thoughts. Don't hold onto them or try to push them away. The content of consciousness comes and goes. You cannot know why it comes or goes. The effort to do so is futile and exhausting.

february 21

The Price of Denial

You can discipline the mind, exercise it like a muscle, even get it to perform magic tricks, but you can never really control its contents. At best, you can focus on certain things and repress others. But what you repress does not go away.

It waits for a moment when you are not on guard and then it takes you hostage. The cost of denying the unsavory aspects of consciousness is much higher than the cost of acknowledging them. How much are you willing to pay to maintain your shaky self-image?

february 22

Needing Attention and Approval

The need for constant attention and approval comes from insecurity. It can destroy a relationship by putting unnatural demands on your partner.

When you ask for more from your partner than s/he is able to give, you set yourself up for disappointment. The solution is to take steps to strengthen yourself and actualize your potential so that you can learn to affirm your self-worth internally.

Then, you don't have to rely inordinately on the approval of your partner to feel good about yourself. Because you are learning to value yourself and express your gifts, your life will naturally generate its own source of support and encouragement.

When you empower yourself, you become capable of giving support as well as receiving it. This will bring balance to your relationship and create the potential for the kind of healthy energy exchanges that occur when both people are living creative lives.

february 23

Planning

It's okay to set goals as long as you aren't foolish enough to believe that you are going to reach them on your timetable and in the manner that you now conceive them. Reality is fluid and changeable. It is not on a fixed course.

No matter how many goals you set and how much you plan, you won't know where you are going until you get there.

feBRuaRy 24

The Miraculous

i t is the nature of the ego to become attached to the past, and to project the past forward into the future. The ego wants what is familiar, because it is basically uncomfortable with change. Its job is to create continuity.

If something is continuous, it is not miraculous. Miraculous events are not continuous with what happened before them. They represent a shift of energy, a movement out of past perception, past limitation. They are unpredictable, unexpected and in many cases inscrutable.

You call them miracles because God's hand is in them. But without your permission, they could not take place. Without your surrender of the past, miracles could not come into your life.

You prepare the ground for them. You create the space in which the miraculous occurs.

feBRuaRy 25

Imaginary Limits

t he limits you create will be real to you until you learn to step beyond them. Then they will cease to be real. Then, you will look back at the reality you used to inhabit and feel claustrophobic, wondering how you were able to stand its narrow confines.

february 26

After Falling in Love

Once upon a time someone appeared on the scene who wanted to love you and take care of you—some contemporary version of the white knight in shining armor or the beautiful damsel in distress—and it was just too tempting for you to refuse. Yet, as you know by now, love's fireworks diminish as the gunpowder runs out. Now, you are lucky if your cherished knight or damsel deigns to peak out from behind the newspaper when you come home at the end of the day! If you are honest, you will see that you too no longer see him/her through rose-colored glasses.

Relationships inevitably become realistic and the fantasy falls apart. And then all you are left with are your natural compatibility and mutual desire for partnership or lack of it. If you have shared interests, a basic "like" for each other, emotional maturity, and realistic expectations, your relationship has a chance of prospering. If not, don't be surprised if "falling in love" leads to "falling out of love."

february 27

The School of Love

It's great to love, but another person's love cannot fill the hole in your heart. Filling up your heart is your responsibility. You need to love and affirm yourself day by day, moment by moment. Without your love for yourself, no amount of love from your partner is enough.

The search for love from other people is like the alcoholic's search for happiness from a bottle. The more he drinks, the less satisfied he feels and the more he wants to drink.

We are all addicted to falling in love. But after we've "fallen" a few times and broken our emotional bones, we hopefully wise up a bit. We know that the high of falling in love is not going to last. We know that sooner or later we will have to get real with each other. That is the difference between romance and partnership.

Romance is an attempt to keep the addiction going. It has a very short half-life. Partnership is the dance of two ordinary people learning to live together day by day. It is a very challenging school that we enroll in. It is sometimes more work than play. And it certainly requires a lot more psychological adjustment than years of therapy! We don't just graduate from this school in a year or two. It takes many years, perhaps even a lifetime, for us to master the curriculum.

february 28

The Plan for Your Awakening

everything that happens to you is part of the plan for your awakening, including those challenging events that force you to shift out of your inertia and self-limiting behavior patterns. From the depth of your soul, you call out for growth. You pray to be released from your burdens and to discover and express your gifts. From deep within your pain you call for peace. From deep within your co-dependency, you call for the courage and the freedom to be yourself.

february 29

Your Greatest Lessons

your greatest lessons are the ones you resist the most. If you have a great deal of resistance to what is happening in your life, there are probably major fears arising that you need to be aware of.

While this may be challenging for you, please realize that it is a time of great spiritual importance. You simply cannot move ahead in your life without becoming conscious of your resistance and beginning to face the fears behind it.

march 1

Unity Consciousness

Only when we accept our entire experience do we move out of duality. The mind that judges, condemns, or engages in selective perception only deeps its experience of conflict. Unity is experienced only when we accept our judgments and forgive them, only when we learn to embrace our entire experience as it is.

march 2

Beauty's Way

Beauty's way is simple and elegant. Everything happens in its own time and place. The river may overflow its banks or it may shrink to a trickle. Seasons of drought and high water are inevitable. But sooner or later, the river will reach the sea. The outcome is certain. No matter how far we stray from our essential nature, we will return to it. Our destiny is to become who we already are.

Our moments of greatest ecstasy and peace are found when we accept ourselves just as we are. In that acceptance, we demonstrate our trust in the river. When we trust the river, it carries us where we need to go.

march 3

Nostalgia and Guilt

Our nostalgia about the past makes what happened seem more palatable than it was when we experienced it. This is one way to avoid the present. Our guilt about the past makes what happened seem worse than it was when we experienced it. This is another way to avoid the present.

march 4

Confessing your Humanity

Don't let your spirituality be a defense against your humanity. Don't try to hide your wounds, your mistakes, your anger, your fear or your sadness in order to win the approval of others. Don't pretend to be someone you are not.

Move away from hiding and secrecy toward self-disclosure and authenticity. Let yourself be seen as you truly are. Confess your mistakes. Share your feelings. Then you can affirm both your humanity and your spirituality.

maRch 5

You are the Judge and the Savior

No one else can condemn you for your mistake or release you from your guilt. You must come to terms with what you have done. You must acknowledge your error and atone for it. The forgiveness of others is nice to have, but it means nothing if you cannot forgive yourself.

maRch 6

Devils and Angels

Each one of us has a devil inside, an angelic being condemned to live in the shadows of our doubts and fears. To acknowledge this dark winged creature is our most courageous act. Each of us must descend to the place where our fears incarnate and face them there. It is not sanitized work. We have to take off our three piece suits and high heel shoes. Work gloves, old jeans, and rubber boots are the dress code of choice.

Our spirituality is not something we gain in the skies. It is something we win in the trenches of daily life. That may not be romantic or consoling. But it is the truth. The sooner we learn it, the easier it will be for us, because we can drop our unrealistic expectations of what it means to be on a spiritual path.

march 7

Facing Our Father Wound

Your father may have given too little or too much. He may have been absent or overbearing, or perhaps a little of both. Whatever he has been, you must come to accept him and see what you have become in your emulation of him or your reaction to him. You must learn to understand him and forgive him. And you must learn to understand and forgive yourself. To know the divine Father, you must come to terms with the human one.

march 8

New Skins for New Wine

We won't be able to break our old dysfunctional patterns if we try to hold onto the securities and paybacks associated with them. As Jesus told us, we can't put new wine into old skins. The old skins must be destroyed. We need new skins for the new wine. We need new forms for our new creations.

MARCH 9

Staying With Our Feelings

Being in a place of peace may be the goal, but if we want to get there we have to engage in the process of being with ourselves when we are not at peace.

When we are angry or sad, we usually try to push our feelings away. Or we try to analyze them, which amounts to the same thing.

Most of us are looking for the rocketship trip to heaven. We want to go from feeling pain to feeling ecstasy without having to change buses. If that's what the journey is about, why are most of the people making progress on the path buying tokens by the bagful?

Perhaps they know something we don't. Perhaps they know it is better to undertake step one in good faith, then to try to leapfrog to step twenty-six on the first attempt.

It takes courage to stay with what we are feeling. And it takes a lot of practice before we can learn to do it effectively.

But what is the alternative? If we insist on denying or intellectualizing our feelings, we will squander the opportunity they provide us for real transformation.

march 10

Divine Mother

i t is time to give and receive nurturing in your life. It is time to stop moving forward with blinders on, attempting to meet your goals and priorities without considering the needs of other people who care about you.

Divine Mother's energy is concerned with the collective vision not the individual one. She is the guardian of the family and the community. She wants what is best for everyone. She often puts her own needs second in order to serve others who need her love or her assistance.

Mother reminds us that we do not live in isolation, but in relationship with other human beings. She asks us to expand our frame of reference to include others, not because she wants us to sacrifice our good, but because she knows our greatest good will be found in union, not in separation.

march 11

Saying No to Manipulation

W hen we say "no" to the attempt of other people to manipulate us, we say "yes" to self-trust. We refuse to be molded into someone else's idea of the way we should be. We move into our own depth. We come to grips with our own resources and learn to trust them. We find our authentic direction and invite the spontaneous flow of grace into our lives.

march 12

Giving our Power Away

When we allow others to control us or we try to dominate them, we do not stand in our own legitimate power. We underextend or overextend ourselves. Either stance weakens us.

If we allow others to carry us, they may pull us off course. If we try to carry others, we may tire and be unable to complete our own journey.

We were given two legs so that we could learn to walk and carry our own baggage. We were not given legs so that we could ride on other people's backs or carry their baggage for them.

march 13

Bringing Love

Every block to love lies in your heart and it is there that it must be dissolved. Don't wait for heaven to come to spread your love around. Do it now. For heaven is in your eyes when you see with acceptance and compassion. It is in your hands when you reach out to help. It is in your mind when you see "good" instead of "evil."

How you see the world determines what the world will be for you. So do not seek to change other people or the world around you. Instead, look at yourself. Look at your beliefs and you will see where you need to bring openness. Look into your own heart and you will know where you need to bring love.

march 14

The Vision Quest

The Self is not a known territory, but a wilderness. Too often we forget that. Too often we reach the boundaries of what we know about ourselves and turn back.

Now is a time to push past those boundaries, to leave behind the old worn-out mask you have been wearing and begin a search for a new definition of who you are and what comes next in your life. Before you venture out, however, you must talk with your people and put things right. Your journey of self discovery must not be an attempt to run away from others. You must leave with your relationships strong and your life intact. Otherwise, your journey will be reactive and you will not open to new wisdom or a new perspective on your life.

march 15

War and Peace

Why do we try to impose our ideas, our values and our beliefs on others? Because we are insecure about our own direction.

This kind of trespass may be inevitable, but we must learn to see it and correct it. We must learn to say "forgive me. I was mistaken. I had no right to impose my ideas on you."

We don't come to peace by trying to change others. We come to peace by being peaceful in our own hearts and minds. The goal of peace and the process of peace are one and the same.

march 16

Keep Finding Love

The foundation of our love is not perfect and it never will be. In places, it is patched, fudged, jerry-rigged. We wonder sometimes how it all holds together. Yet it does. It does because we want it to, because each day we are willing to do what the relationship asks of us, even if we sometimes do it kicking and screaming. It does because we keep finding love, even as we move awkwardly and sadly through the pain. It does because we know and trust that our partner will be there for us, no matter what.

That is not something we know right away. That is not something we can promise in advance. It is something that happens in its own time.

march 17

Empty Promises

Your life is your spiritual path. Don't be quick to abandon it for promises of bigger and better experiences. You are getting exactly the experiences you need to grow. If your growth seems too slow or uneventful for you, it is because you have not fully embraced the situations and relationships at hand.

march 18

Taking off the Mask

the personality and behavior patterns you are reacting to are just a mask. If you see only the mask, you won't see who the other person is. If s/he sees only your mask, s/he will not see you truly.

march 19

The Wrong Choice?

You think your problem lies in making the wrong choice. But that is absurd. Every choice is an opportunity to learn. It cannot be wrong, unless your refuse to learn from your mistakes.

march 20

The Power of Light

Light does not resist or avoid darkness. It merely includes it, welcomes it, and loves it. Thus, darkness disappears into the light.

Light is not afraid of the shadow for it knows the appearance of the shadow is the first sign of illumination. When we see the shadow, we no longer have to be afraid of it. When the shadow cannot provoke our fear, it has no power to undermine us.

march 21

Christ and Anti-Christ

Both Christ and Anti-Christ live within the mind of every man and woman. Christ is the collective Spirit, the force for love and joining. Anti-Christ is the collective ego, the force of fear and separation. Christ liberates. Anti-Christ binds. Christ trusts his brother and sets him free to make mistakes and learn with confidence in the outcome. Anti-Christ distrust his brother's motives, seeks to influence his choice and lives in constant fear of betrayal.

Christ offers salvation to all right now. Anti-Christ preaches salvation only to a chosen few. Christ preaches the message of divine love and the potential of creating heaven on earth. Anti-Christ preaches divine retribution, the imminent end of the world, and happiness only in the afterlife.

Christ is the voice of love. Anti-Christ is the voice of fear.

march 22

Opposing Falsehood

That which opposes the darkness is not light, but another form of darkness. That which opposes fear is not love but another form of fear.

Truth does not oppose falsehood. It waits patiently, quietly, yet with open arms.

march 23

The Right Packaging?

*Y*ou might not recognize that your prayers have been answered if you pay too much attention to the package the gift comes in. Some of the most important gifts come badly wrapped. Indeed, at first sight, you might question whether they are gifts at all.

Better not to ask for the gift than to be attached to the way in which it comes to you. The statement "Ask and you will receive" is true only when you are completely open to the form in which the gift may appear.

march 24

The Path to Happiness

*t*he purveyors of spiritual growth tell you that following their methods will lead you to happiness. Some of them are very good at marketing. Their advertisements are seductive and convincing. But following their methods doesn't lead to happiness any more than drinking the featured alcoholic drink gets you the beautiful woman or handsome man in the commercial.

You don't have to "do" anything, "buy" anything or "drink" anything to be happy. There is no path to happiness. Happiness itself is the path.

march 25

Ghosts and Goblins

Don't waste your time doing battle with the people who push your buttons. Don't take their attacks on you personally or you will be drawn into a vicious cycle of attack and defense. You don't need to prove them wrong or prove yourself right.

People who anger you are like ghosts passing in the night. Let them pass, but look carefully as they go by. The only reality they have is to show you your own fears.

march 26

Surrender

As long as you think it has to be "your way," you haven't gotten it! You can't have control if you want to live a life of Spirit. Spirituality requires surrender.

You aren't asked to surrender to someone else, nor are you asked to capitulate to your own ego. You are asked to surrender to the River that lies within you.

The River is in charge. Your only choice is to fight its authority (an exhausting choice) or to surrender to it. Some people figure out right away that surrender is inevitable. For others, it takes years.

march 27

Defense Mechanisms are Energy Drains

We all put far too much energy into our defensive, self-protective rituals. When we stop doing this, we release an unbelievable amount of energy into our lives. And the more energy we put out, the more returns to us.

Doors that we once knocked on in vain now spontaneously open to us. Opportunities that once recoiled from us now walk up to us and shake us by the hand.

march 28

Separation or Joining

Each moment offers us a choice of whether to separate or join. That is the only choice we have faced before and the only choice we will ever face. Unfortunately, we do not remember the pain of separation or the bliss of joining. That is why we have come to this place together, to help each other remember.

march 29

Clear Discrimination

A loving person does not perpetuate attack in any guise. Her unconditional acceptance of each person enables her to discriminate clearly without taking sides.

MARCH 30

Love's Patient Blessing

Wherever you go, the love of God goes with you. It moves with your legs, reaches with your hands, speaks with your voice and sees with your eyes.

Because of you, love goes forth into the world. Without you, it would be invisible.

The love that expresses through you is the Holy Presence, the human vehicle ablaze with the divine light, the very embodiment of God's love.

You hear the call, and you answer it by following this simple teaching: "Whatever is not loving must be forgiven; and what is forgiven becomes love's patient blessing on an imperfect world."

MARCH 31

Defenselessness

When you see that the source of the problem lies within, you look inward and discover how to remove the blocks to love in your heart. When you see that other people are the obstacle, you learn to step gently around them and offer love instead.

april 1

Battling Egos

Your ego will always be in conflict with other egos. Your job is to observe this, not to try to overcome the other person's ego or to try to make your ego go away.

april 2

Words can be Divisive

Words have the power you give them. Sometimes, it isn't wise to take them too seriously. People don't always do what they say they will do. Wait and see if the words will scatter or take root. Words said in anger or haste can be forgiven and forgotten. Only when such words translate into actions do you need to take them seriously.

Until then, don't let words divide you into separate camps. There is only one camp.

april 3

Justice and Injustice

every mistake will eventually be brought to truth. Be patient. Others will learn their lessons in time. Don't try to take justice into your hands or you will deepen your pain and that of others.

An angry person cannot stand up for truth. As long as you are angry, you must deal with your anger. Only when your sword has been transformed into a plowshare does your commitment to truth become constructive.

Until that time, allow the truth to uphold itself. There is nothing here you need to protect or defend.

april 4

The Perception of Inequality

don't try to justify your judgments or prejudices. Judgment is judgment; prejudice is prejudice. There is nothing noble or justifiable about them. Don't try to disguise them under a cloak of self-righteousness. Every perception of inequality requires correction and forgiveness. There are no exceptions.

apriL 5

Row the Boat

Some people complain about the boat. Others try to escape it. Neither choice is helpful.

Until you accept the boat for what it is, it cannot take you to the other side.

apriL 6

The Gift of Listening

We believe that we listen, but it's not true. Listening, if we did it deeply and fully, would transform our lives.

Listening is an experience of communion when we choose to be present, when we "hear" with our heart and not just with our ears. Listening is not a casual or insignificant act, but an act of great purpose and beauty, an act that will inspire and uplift. It is a way that we can offer each other love and respect.

We listen not to agree or to disagree, but simply to hear each other's experience. And we speak not to obtain attention or approval, but to communicate what is in our hearts and minds.

Our greatest joy is not to find agreement with others, but to experience hearing and being heard deeply and without judgment. This outcome can be achieved in every encounter.

april 7

Throw Away Your Pictures

When you are centered in yourself, any road you travel is acceptable. There is no reason to try to manipulate the journey to bring you to some magical destination, because no place is any more important than any other place.

When you realize the light within, that light shines equally on everyone you meet. You don't steer toward certain people and away from others.

You throw away your stash of pictures of the "ideal beloved" and love the person in front of you. You don't waste your time resisting reality or trying to change it. You embrace it as it is.

april 8

Committing to the Goal

All you can do is understand the goal and commit to it in each moment. Unless you commit to the goal in a consistent manner, the means to reach it will not be found.

apriL 9

The Voice of Fear and the Voice of Love

the voice of fear would have us believe that nothing is right or acceptable the way it is. Everything needs to revised, tweaked, fixed, changed, redeemed, and transformed. The voice of love reassures us that everything is fine just the way it is. We need only accept it and work with it to the best of our ability.

apriL 10

Your Brother's Call for Help

you can walk on one leg, but it is not as efficient as walking on two. You can live a solitary life, but you won't grow as much spiritually as you will if you become involved with other people.

To be alone is essential, but never sufficient. No matter how solitary you become, you cannot escape your brother's call for help. To try to do so is foolish. For it is his call for help that forces you to look at your own anger, fear and guilt.

april 11

Learning to say No Clearly

When you don't want to do something, say "no" clearly. Ambivalence here leads to a scenario of self-betrayal and inappropriate blaming of others.

A simple "no" said clearly from the heart can prevent the drama of self-abuse. Others who are drawn into our dramas have their own lessons in this area, but it is pointless to try to teach them or correct them. We need to address this issue in ourselves.

When we no longer betray ourselves by saying "yes" when we want to say "no", we will no longer attract people who disrespect our boundaries, nor will others feel betrayed by us when they discover that our "yes" was not an authentic "yes" but a "no" pretending to be a "yes."

april 12

Not Loving Yourself

Love offers blessing not blame. Whenever you interpret your experience negatively, you are not loving yourself. This is true whether you blame others or blame yourself.

april 13

Who Holds the Child?

Beyond your judgment and your fear, there is one who understands and forgives, who holds everything that happens in your life with great compassion. S/he is the one who embraces and calms the wounded child awakened from its nightmarish dreams. In her loving arms, the screams of the child diminish. Terror disappears and safety returns.

You are the both the child kicking and screaming and the one who holds that child with compassion. You are the one who cries out desperately for safety and for love and the one who confidently answers the call.

april 14

Awareness

Beneath the judgment layer of the mind is the witness who sees what is going on without judging it. The witness neither resists thoughts nor identifies with them, but simply observes them as they come and go, with all their elaborate interpretations and justifications.

When we get quiet, we become the witness. Thoughts come and go, but we know that we are not those thoughts. We begin to rest in something larger than thought, something that holds those thoughts compassionately. You can call it awareness. You can call it silence. It is the place from which thoughts spring and to which they return. There, mind is clear, like the surface of a lake when there is no wind. There, mind is at peace.

april 15

An Open Mind

Peace and clarity are the attributes of an open mind. An open mind does not cherish opinions or harbor prejudices. It is not preoccupied with judgments or interpretations.

An open mind is unfettered and free to respond to the challenges of the moment. It does not dwell on the past or fantasize about the future. It is present right here and now. As a result, it is open to all of the possibilities that might arise.

april 16

Resting in the Storm

When we are feeling tense or pressured our internal barometer begins to rise and we can sense a storm brewing. At such times, we need to take the pressure off, take a deep breath and just let things be. If we do this as soon as we notice our distress, we may be able to reduce the pressure enough that the storm subsides or blows out to sea.

Sometimes, there is nothing we can do to avoid the brunt of the storm. When that happens, we need to weather the storm courageously. We need to remember that no matter how hard the rain falls or the wind blows there is blue sky and sunlight behind the clouds.

Troubled though we may be, we are more than just the storm. We are also the sky in which the storm appears.

april 17

A Healthy Relationship with Our Fear

We have an unhealthy relationship with our fear when we allow it to prevent us from taking risks that are essential to our growth or when we ignore our fear and insist on taking risks we are not ready to take. We need to avoid these extremes.

We have a healthy relationship with our fear when we acknowledge it when it comes up, without giving it permission to run our lives. We may take a step or two back when we feel overwhelmed, but then we take several steps forward toward our goal. We don't stay stuck in one place, nor do we venture out completely unprepared for the conditions we might face. We take reasonable and appropriate risks. Little by little, we stretch our comfort zones

april 18

You can't Pry Open The Heart

A broken heart needs time to mend. You need to learn to trust other people gradually. You can't rush things. You have paid for your impulsiveness in the past by getting hurt and then shutting down emotionally. If you don't have some discipline and restraint, you might do the same thing again.

So go slowly. Go gently. The heart does not have to be pried open. It opens naturally if you give it time.

april 19

Attachment to an Outcome

Your attachment to specific results puts pressure on yourself and others. It makes it difficult for things to unfold naturally. If you want to experience less struggle in your life, let go of your attachment to a specific outcome and allow things to unfold organically. Then, you may be surprised at how much better things turn out than you expect them to.

april 20

Feeling Overwhelmed

Sometimes our feelings overwhelm us. But that is usually because we are afraid of them and try to push them away. Instead of resisting the feeling and trying to make it go away, try breathing into it. Use the breath to establish a place of peace from which you may begin to be with your feelings, accept them, and learn from them.

april 21

A Blessing in Disguise

Life has its ups and downs, its ebb and its flow. The same variation can be found in our own consciousness. Sometimes we are joyful. Other times we are sad. Sometimes we are confident and loving; other times we are fearful and defensive.

When we are patient and look deeply, we see that things are constantly changing, both in the outside world and in our own consciousness. Peaks become valleys. Sadness yields to joy. What seems like failure turns out to be a blessing in disguise.

april 22

If Love Isn't Happening Now

It doesn't matter how many times you have read the sacred scrolls. It doesn't matter how many mantras or prayers you said yesterday or the day before. If love isn't happening right now, it isn't happening. It doesn't matter how many Buddhas or Christs have come before you.

april 23

The Need for Tribal Education

The answers to our school problems are not going to be found in throwing more dollars at them or in building bigger schools. We need to realize that bigger is not necessarily better and spending more may actually lead to less quality: unpopular propositions perhaps, but ones we must begin to face.

The answer will be found in rebuilding our tribal society, consisting of many small, diverse social groupings where kids feel loved and connected. It will be places where mom—or someone pretending to be mom—and dad—or someone pretending to be dad—is home. That's where kids will feel safe and that's where they will learn the most.

It's not a quick fix. But surely we knew it couldn't be.

april 24

Resting

Periods of rest and relaxation are as important to the well being of our consciousness as are periods of activity. Rest supports activity. Activity necessitates rest.

One of the keys to living a life filled with grace is understanding when we need to rest and when we need to work, when we need to be alone and when we need to be with others, when we need to give and when we need to receive.

april 25

Waiting for the Fruit

Flowers can be seductive and overwhelming. They often promise more than they deliver.

The wise person smells the flower, but waits for the fruit. S/he pays more attention to actions than to words.

april 26

Finding God

Seeking God is a set up. It inevitably leads to a cul de sac. You cannot find God somewhere out there in the world, because God does not exist apart from you.

Whatever God is, you are potentially that. The divine spark is inside you. If you do not see that potential in yourself and in your brothers and sisters, what good does it do to seek God? Do you really think you will find God as some entity separate from your consciousness?

april 27

Love Never Chooses Sides

When your mind is in conflict, you do not move out of conflict by choosing between two opposing positions. That will just set up more intense conflict. You move out of conflict by accepting both positions.

Love never chooses one brother over another. It never sees one sister as better or more worthy than another. It affirms the humanity of both.

If positive and negative feelings are present, love does not reject one and embrace the other. It accepts that both are present. It embraces the totality of what is, with all its apparent contradiction.

Love transcends any kind of dualism. It is many-sided, multifaceted, patient and tolerant. It knows that we will be okay. It trusts us to learn what we need to learn when we are ready to learn it.

april 28

Something New, Something Old

Food needs an empty stomach. Truth needs an empty mind. For something new to come in, something old must be released.

april 29

True Wisdom

to know that you don't know is true wisdom. Thinking you know when you don't is the major obstacle to realizing truth.

april 30

You Don't Have the Wrong Horse

Please stop complaining and finding fault with your life. Experiment; try a different approach! For thirty days, practice finding something positive in everything that happens to you.

Don't "romanticize" your life or pretend that you are happy when you aren't. If you are not happy, recognize it and ask "What is positive about my unhappiness?"

Life is your horse, but you aren't riding it. Get up in the saddle and stay on it for 30 days. Don't stop riding because you think you have the wrong horse. You don't have the wrong horse, so don't try to trade your horse for a better one. That never works.

Only the horse you are riding will take you where you need to go. Trust it and care for it. And see what happens.

One more hint: If you lead your horse to water and he won't drink, don't worry. He just isn't thirsty. When he needs a drink, he will find the stream before you do.

may 1

Giving without Resentment

We may think that we are being generous to others, but when we resent them for not expressing their gratitude or giving back to us, we need to question our own motives.

Did we give unconditionally or did we give to get something back? Did we feel good in giving or did we feel that we were making a sacrifice?

Only our honesty here can tell us whether or not our gift was genuine. If it was, we won't resent it. If we resent it, chances are the gift was not given freely.

may 2

Heaven on Earth

Heaven on earth means you are absolutely delighted with your life just the way it is. You aren't trying to fix yourself or manifest more money, a better job or a bigger house. You find the sacred right here and right now. That is also where you connect with the creative energy that wants to express in your life.

Abundance comes as you learn to trust the Creative source inside of you. You can't do that when you are busy finding fault with your life.

may 3

Forgiving Sin and Violation

We cannot condone the action of someone who commits an unnatural act. But we can feel compassion for the soul of the person who commits this act and for the soul of the victim(s).

When someone commits a perverse act, we must decide if we will answer injustice with injustice or with compassion. When we allow ourselves to feel compassion, we feel the pain of both victim and victimizer. We feel the collective wound within our own hearts. If we do not feel the pain on both sides of the wound, we cannot heal from it, individually or collectively.

may 4

The Body of Truth

The Body of Truth is one indivisible body. All beings belong to It. All falsehood and deception is a refusal to see and accept the Body of Truth.

You cannot accept the Body of Truth for yourself and deny another's right to It, nor can you deny your right and accept someone else's.

The Body of Truth has many names. It is the Body of Christ, Para-Brahman, Tao, Dharmakaya, and so on. Names do not matter.

All scripture is a key that opens the door to the heart. Once that door opens, truth is no longer something to be talked about. It is embodied in each moment.

It offers only love, without conditions, embracing all.

may 5

Unity Consciousness

S ometimes words get so confusing you just have to toss them away and get quiet. It doesn't matter what you call it when you get quiet. Call it being. Call it witnessing. Call it time-out. The idea is to sink down beneath the layer of mind that wants to define everything and know what to expect from life before it happens.

Unity consciousness is not dualistic or exclusive. In unity consciousness, black and white are mutually valid assumptions, and there are infinite shades of gray. It is inclusive. You can "be" and "do" simultaneously.

People ask for a step by step approach to unity consciousness, but all you can give them is step one: get quiet. Turn your attention inward. Breathe and be. The rest will take care of itself.

may 6

Experiential Learning

W e are always trying to understand what we are going to experience before we experience it. But this is not experiential learning. It is intellectual learning.

Experiential learning happens when you open to an experience without knowing what is going to happen. Then you find out what that experience is. And often what happens is not at all what you thought would happen.

You can ask questions about many subjects, including about meditation or spirituality, but the real answers will not arise until after you allow the experience to take place.

may 7

Your Essence

Don't romanticize your wounds or make an identity out of your disability or dis-ease. Wounds exist to reawaken wholeness. Illness happens to create awareness of health. No matter how broken you may feel, your essence is whole, dynamic, and free. It but awaits your trust.

may 8

Incomparable

Do not compare yourself to others. Their light does not impede or diminish the light in you.

You are one facet in the many-faceted jewel of God's love and grace. The beauty of one facet does not interfere with the splendor of another, but adds to it in both breadth and intensity.

may 9

The Fountainhead

Look to the example of the great teachers within your spiritual tradition not to worship them, but to understand what is possible for you. Drink deeply from the well of their love, for tomorrow you will be the fountain. You will be the one who is called upon to offer love without conditions.

may 10

Hiding the Truth from Yourself

The only thing that is easier than deceiving others is deceiving yourself. You may be a master at taking truth and inverting it, but just because you have inverted truth does not mean the truth ceases to be true. It means only that you have succeeded in hiding the truth from yourself.

may 11

Meeting Your Fear with Compassion

When you are feeling fearful, your only constructive course of action is to recognize your fear, realize that you are incapable of making good decisions, and begin to work on accepting your fear and moving through it.

Here are four simple steps that can help you do this:

1. Recognize your fear. Notice the signs that fear is coming up for you: shallow breathing, pounding heart, nervousness, anxiety, attack thoughts, anger.

2. Recognize that the solution your ego offers is motivated by fear and it can't bring you peace.

3. Accept your fear. Get your arms around all of it. Say to yourself "It's okay that I'm afraid." Don't try to make the fear go away. Be gentle with yourself and try to tune into why fear is coming up for you.

4. Tell yourself "I don't have to decide anything now. I can wait until my fear subsides to make any decisions that need to be made."

may 12

A Single Idea

all great spiritual teachings have been distorted by people who lack the inspiration, wisdom and compassion of the original teacher. Even today, this desecration of the teaching continues. That is why you must be vigilant.

Yet, do not let your vigilance and healthy skepticism make you narrow minded or fearful about new, creative approaches. That would prevent the teaching from being renewed and reinvigorated, as it must be to remain relevant to each new generation of people.

Consider what is said in the depths of your heart and ask there if it is true or false. A single false idea can bring the mind that thinks it to despair. But a single true thought restores the kingdom.

may 13

Truth is an Open Door

truth is a door that remains open. You cannot close this door. You can choose not to enter. You can walk in the opposite direction. But you can never say: "I tried to enter, but the door was closed." The door is never closed to you or anyone else.

may 14

Lifting the Veil

i t is not necessary for you to try to be more spiritual. You are already spiritual enough.

You already have God's love. You just need to dissolve the blocks to your awareness of it

Please question all judgments and thoughts that do not bless you and others. These stand in the way of your ability to give and receive love.

As your awareness of these blocks increases, they will begin to dissolve. Your job is not to try to change what you see, but to lift the veil so that you can see more clearly.

may 15

Humpty Dumpty

i f you are a student of Murphy's Law you know that it is utterly amazing that anything in the universe functions with any kind of order or regularity. This is especially true when it has to do with the behavior of human beings.

The question for you is not "Why does Humpty Dumpty come off the Wall?" but "Why do you keep putting him back up there?"

may 16

Stop Pretending

a s illusions are surrendered, truth reappears. As separation is relinquished, the original unity re-emerges unchanged. When you stop pretending to be what you are not, what you are can be clearly seen.

may 17

A Journey toward Light

t he light of truth lives even in the darkest of places. There is no such thing as total absence of light. Darkness cannot exist except in reference to the light. No matter how great your pain, it is measured in the degree to which you feel the love's absence or loss. All darkness is a journey toward light. All pain is a journey toward love without conditions

may 18

Perceiving our Wholeness

each one of us is whole. We already have integrity. We don't have to look for it somewhere outside ourselves.

The problem is that we believe that we are not whole. We believe that we need to be fixed or that we can fix someone else. We feel a false sense of responsibility for others and we do not take enough responsibility for ourselves. We attack, defend, and then try to repair the damage. Of course, it doesn't work.

In truth, nothing is broken and nothing needs to be fixed. If we could dwell in this awareness, our psychic wounds would heal by themselves. We would realize that we have never been victims and that we have never lacked for anything we truly needed.

When we accept ourselves and affirm our wholeness, the person finding fault with our lives—whether it is an inner or an outer critic—moves out of the way.

may 19

The Spark of Divine Light

you can forget about the original spark of divine light that was entrusted to you, but you cannot give it back. You can ignore or deny it, but you cannot destroy it. The deeper the darkness through which you walk, the more visible the tiny spark becomes. Like a beacon, it calls to you, reminding you of your essence and your place of origin.

may 20

Walking in Peace

Words and beliefs that separate you from others must be put aside. If you wish to walk in peace, find what you share with others and overlook the differences you see.

may 21

White Knights have Dark Shadows

When you continue to attract partners who promise you the world and then betray you, you might begin to wonder why you are punishing yourself.

The next time the white knight appears at your doorstep, you should remember that it's really the bogeyman in disguise.

Of course, if you overlook the dark shadow behind him and stare vainly into his shining armor, then you will be taking yourself for another ride.

Don't blame the knight or the bogeyman. This is about you.

may 22

Truth Appears in Many Forms

God has many ways of bringing us home. Do not think that those who follow a different path home will be denied salvation. Truth comes in all shapes and sizes, but it remains one simple truth. You must learn to see the truth in every form, in each situation.

may 23

Admitting Your Mistakes

Being aware of your mistakes is a gift because it brings you to correction.

When you justify your mistakes, you hang onto them, forcing yourself to defend your actions over and over again. This takes a great deal of time and energy. Indeed, if you are not careful, it can become the dominant theme of your life.

When you admit your mistakes, you deliver yourself from these rituals of deceit. You begin to move toward correction.

You may be ashamed of your mistake, but don't think it can't be corrected. You may feel terrible about your trespass, but don't think that you can't atone for it. If you want forgiveness, you have to have the courage to ask for it.

may 24

Correction

To be mistaken is not so terrible a thing. It will not deprive you of love and acceptance. What deprives you of love is your insistence on being right when you are not. That prevents correction from being made.

may 25

Dancing With the Past

Do not gather wood unless you want to make a fire. Do not stir the pot unless you want to smell the stew. Do not solicit the past unless you want to dance with it.

But if there is a fire in your house, you must pick up your things and leave. If the stew is boiling, you can't help but smell it. If the past is dancing in your mirror, you can't pretend to be in samadhi.

Resistance of experience creates endless detours. But so does seeking. Do not resist. Do not seek. Just deal with what comes up as it happens.

may 26

Making Others Wrong

To make wrong is to teach guilt and perpetuate the belief that punishment is necessary. To make right is to teach love and demonstrate forgiveness. To put it simply, you are never right to make wrong, or wrong to make right. To be right, make right.

You cannot love in an unloving way. You can't be right and attack what's wrong.

may 27

Forgiving Yourself

L earn to forgive yourself. No matter what you have said or done, you do not deserve to suffer. Your suffering will not feed the hungry or heal the sick.

Forgive and come back into your life with a clear vision and a strong heart. Your freedom from guilt serves not just you, but also those who need your kind deeds and your compassionate understanding.

may 28

Your Greatest Good

R emember, your good and that of your brother or sister are one and the same. You cannot advance your life by hurting another, nor can you help another by hurting yourself. All attempts to break this simple equation lead to suffering and despair.

may 29

Withholding Love

O nly by recognizing the worth of others is your own worth confirmed. When you withhold your love, your enemy is not the only one who is denied that blessing. You are denied it too.

may 30

True Giving

true giving is an overflowing of your love. You don't feel that you are being depleted when you give in this way. In fact, you feel energized, because the love you give away returns to you through the gratitude of the people you have touched.

may 31

Loving Your Enemy

You might think that your enemy is blocking your access to the love you want when, in fact, s/he is the doorway to the Source of that love.

Your enemy is your ally in disguise. Making peace with him or her leads to peace within your own heart and mind.

Your ability to love your enemy demonstrates your willingness to look at all of the dark places within your mind. Your enemy is a mirror into which you look until the angry face that you see smiles back at you.

june 1

Messages from Spirit

Don't be surprised if Spirit addresses you when you get quiet. It would be more surprising if you were not addressed. Since Spirit doesn't usually get many opportunities to get your attention, it usually takes advantage of the opportunities it gets.

Messages from the Spirit are uplifting, inspiring, centering, encouraging. They do not complicate or confuse us, but simplify our lives and make straight our path. They make it easier for us to love ourselves and others.

june 2

Freedom from Violence

You cannot stop hatred by fighting it with revenge. Every act of violence begets a counter-act. The only approach that can bring freedom from violence is one that is itself free of violence. Only a spiritual solution works.

june 3

Modeling Love

Preaching to others is rarely successful. Words of love require confirmatory actions. If you preach love and act in a fearful way, people are not inspired by your example.

If you want someone to act in a loving way, you must be willing to love him. Only your love for him will teach him the meaning of love.

june 4

Keys to the Kingdom

Forgiveness is an internal proposition. When we realize that there is only one person to forgive in any situation and that is ourselves, we finally understand that we have been given the keys to the Kingdom.

june 5

Love Without Conditions

When you love without conditions, you support the freedom of others to choose their own way, even when you disagree with them. You trust them to make the best choice for them. You trust God's plan for their awakening. You know that they can never make a mistake that will cut them off from God's love or from yours.

june 6

Coming Face to Face

the truth is that you can be only as happy with another person as you can be with yourself. If you like who you are, being with another person can be an extension of your happiness. But, if you do not like yourself, being with someone else can only exacerbate your unhappiness.

Your decision to enter into partnership should not be based on a desire to avoid looking at yourself, but on a willingness to intensify that process. When you live with other people, you are likely to trigger their unhealed wounds and they are likely to trigger yours. Becoming aware of the unhealed parts of you is neither pleasant nor easy. However, it is a necessary part of the journey to psychic wholeness.

Relationship is like a giant backhoe. It digs down through the superficial layers of consciousness and exposes your deepest fears and insecurities. If you aren't willing to look this deeply, you might want to question your desire to be in an intimate relationship. You can't get close to another person without coming face to face with yourself.

june 7

Committing to Loving Yourself

unless you commit to loving yourself, others can offer you only detours, side-trips, running in place. Time goes by, but nothing changes. The pain doesn't lift. The pattern of self- betrayal remains.

june 8

Forgiveness Helps us Release the Past

O ur relationships are easily crippled by their own past baggage. When anger and hurt are carried around, there is an undercurrent of judgment and irritation that surfaces when new challenges arise. Even little problems become major issues.

The air needs to be cleared. The burden of past misunderstandings needs to be laid to rest.

Forgiveness is not a doing so much as it is an undoing. It enables us to undo blame and guilt. It wipes the slate clean of resentment. It enables us to start fresh with each other so that we don't have to keep carrying the trauma of the past around with us.

june 9

Fear of Intimacy

P eople who are afraid of love are ambivalent about giving and receiving. When you are aloof, they feel safe and desire your presence. But when you come close, they get scared and ask you to back off or go away. This emotionally teasing behavior enables them to be in relationship while avoiding intimacy and commitment.

If you are drawn into such a relationship, you must face the fact that you too may be afraid to receive love. Why else would you choose a partner who cannot give it?

june 10

Marriage

m arriage is not a promise to be together throughout all eternity, for no one can promise that. It is a promise to be present "now." It is a vow that must be renewed in each moment if it is to have meaning.

june 11

Real Love

f orgiveness is the key to success in every relationship. If you and your partner are committed to practicing forgiveness, you can live together successfully, even if you don't have a lot in common. On the other hand, if the two of you are not willing to practice forgiveness, then nothing you try will work. No, not religion, or psychotherapy, or relationship workshops.

Through the practice of forgiveness, imperfect people become whole, and broken relationships are healed and strengthened. You learn what real love and real essence are all about.

june 12

Ending an Agreement

When one person no longer wants to keep an agreement, the agreement is off. You can't hold someone against his or her will. If you try to do so, you will push love away.

Love survives the ending of agreements, if you will allow it to. If you won't, you only cheat yourself.

june 13

Conditional Love

Your experience of love will be diminished in direct proportion to your need to control it. Control places conditions upon that which must be without conditions. When you establish conditions on love, you experience the conditions, not the love.

june 14

True Detachment

True detachment comes from familiarity with others, not from estrangement. Distancing others does not bring detachment, but its opposite. Only when you let others into your heart do you become capable of releasing them.

june 15

Telling the Truth about Our Experience

truth, like freedom, always carries a price. But the price of not telling the truth is much higher.

Not telling the truth may give us temporary security, but it is the security of a prison. We get a bed to lie on and food to eat, but we never get to see what lies behind the prison walls.

Each one of us has a unique journey. Even if we travel a well worn path, we must go at our own pace and have our own experiences. We cannot do this if we let others rush us or hold us back.

When we are feeling uncomfortable with the direction or the pace, we need to speak up. Our journey will be authentic and true only if we have the courage to be honest about who we are.

june 16

Your Life is a Work of Art

your life is a work of art and you need to be busy about it even as a bee is busy pollinating flowers. But please remember that work that is not joyful to you accomplishes nothing of value in the world.

june 17

The Gifts of God

T he gifts of God do not feed your ego expectations. Their value is of a higher order. They help you open to your true nature and purpose here.

Sometimes they seem to close a door and you don't understand why. Only when the right door opens do you understand why the wrong door was closed.

june 18

What you Love Prospers

W hat you deeply value has your loving attention. It is nurtured, watered, and brought into fullness. It does not happen overnight. It does not happen exactly how or when you want it to. But it does come into being when conditions are right. And, after that, it requires your continued commitment to grow and to flourish.

june 19

Giving Your Gift

o not make the mistake of thinking that you have no gift to give. Everyone has a gift.

Your gift brings joy to yourself and to others. It helps you step forward and express yourself. It breaks down the barriers of separation, helps you connect with others, and allows other people to know who you are.

june 20

Waiting for the Perfect Pitch

he best hitters are patient, but realistic. They know that they aren't going to get a perfect pitch to hit. So they swing at anything that will get them on base and move other base-runners over. They are content to play their part. They know they don't have to win the game by themselves.

The way you relate to your gift says a lot about whether you are happy or not. Happy people are expressing their gifts on whatever level and in whatever arena life offers them. They do all the little things necessary to build momentum. Unhappy people are holding onto their gifts until life gives them the perfect opportunity. They try to hit a home-run every time they come to the plate. They strike out repeatedly and leave a lot of baserunners stranded.

june 21

True Prosperity

Do not cheat yourself by working out of sacrifice. Do not cheat others by working out of greed.

Do not deny yourself what you need to live with dignity. Yet be respectful of the needs of others and do not take more than you need.

Find a balance between meeting your material needs and your spiritual needs. That is what true prosperity means.

june 22

The Dance of Energy

When two people approach each other weak or needy, wanting attention or approval, both will be disappointed. That is because neither person is in a position to give.

To give, we must be feeling good about ourselves. Then our goodness naturally extends to others.

When others ask us to dance, our dance with ourselves intensifies. We need to take time to love and nurture ourselves or we won't have the strength to support others when they need our help.

june 23

Spiritual Rewards

there is no more truth in the religion of abundance than there is in the religion of sacrifice. God does not necessarily reward spiritual work with material success. All rewards are spiritual. Happiness, joy, compassion, peace, sensitivity: these are the rewards for a life lived in integrity.

You must learn, once and for all, to stop measuring spiritual riches with a worldly yardstick. Your lifework can be profoundly successful even if it doesn't bring in a large paycheck.

june 24

Sharing Your Wealth

on't make the mistake of thinking that you must be poor to serve God. A rich person can serve God as well as a person of humble means if he is willing to share his riches. It doesn't matter how much you hold in your hands as long as your hands are extended outward to your brother or sister.

june 25

Lack of Clarity Leads to Mixed Results

When you say "yes" to what you want and "no" to what you don't want, you tend to bring into your life what you ask for. However, when you don't know what you want or when you know but don't trust it, the results are often weak or inconclusive.

When you are ambivalent or in conflict, you cannot manifest clearly or abundantly. Moreover, when your unconscious desires are different from your conscious goals, what you bring into your life reflects a mixture of both.

june 26

Experiencing Joy

You cannot experience joy in life by following or opposing the ideas and actions of other people. You experience joy only by remaining faithful to the truth within your own heart.

june 27

Spiritual Focus

o not focus on what is missing but on what is always there and cannot be taken away. Do not focus on what is wrong or bad, but on what is right and good.

Because you do not look for weaknesses, you will help people find their strength. Because you do not look for wounds, you will help people find their gratitude.

june 28

Ministry of Love

minister of love does not proselytize or aggressively spread the message. S/he just loves and accepts people and they keep coming back. That is the way the teaching is extended.

Being a minister of love requires honesty and humility. You keep admitting your mistakes and confessing your worries and fears, and people hold you ever more deeply in their hearts.

june 29

Opening to Each Other

Don't worry about how long your relationship is going to last. Just give it your best energy and attention. Experience as much joy as you can with your partner. Learn as much as you can from the painful times. Do your best to be honest and clear with each other. Stretch your comfort zones a little. Be flexible and constructive. Be the first to yield and to bless. Give without worrying about what you are going to get back. And when you fall down, get back up and laugh at your own stupidity.

You will never be perfect in your ability to give or receive love. Don't try to be. Just try to be a little more open today than you were yesterday.

june 30

Scarcity

Don't think that you aren't worthy of acceptance and love just because you did not receive the material results you were expecting. The experience of scarcity is not God punishing you. It is you showing yourself a belief that needs to be corrected.

juLy 1

Connecting to Love

When you enter a beautiful forest, you do not say "only the birch trees are beautiful" or "the maples are better than the oaks." You admire the beauty and diversity of all the trees in the forest.

People who think their religion is better than other religions are missing the beauty of diversity. Each religion has a unique character that enables it to speak to certain people and not to others.

If we don't respect other traditions, we will weaken our own. Our narrowness and prejudice will be obvious to all who listen to us. Only by treating people of other faiths with love and acceptance will we give our tradition a good name.

Indeed, only by connecting to the core teaching of love within our tradition can we pass that teaching on to our children. A barren tree will make no fruit. A religion that does not help its followers connect to love will not prosper.

juLy 2

Abundance

You will not increase your happiness just by increasing your material possessions. You increase your happiness only by increasing your energy, your self-expression and your love.

The goal in life should not be to accumulate resources that you don't need and cannot possibly use. It should be to earn what you need, enjoy and can share joyfully with others.

juLy 3

Giving and Receiving

You can give only what you believe that you have and you can receive only what you believe you deserve. If you try to give something you don't believe you have, others will sense that your gift is insincere and they won't want to accept it. If you try to receive something you don't think you deserve, you will place so many conditions on the gift that you make it impossible for others to give it to you.

Such aborted attempts at giving and receiving can be emotionally exhausting. They can also weaken your self confidence so that you go into the next experience expecting failure.

It's better to slow down and get honest with yourself. Then, you can be honest with others.

If you don't believe you have the gift, don't try to give it. If you don't believe you deserve the gift, don't try to receive it. Wait until you are ready to give the gift and to receive it, and you will have much better chance of succeeding.

juLy 4

Selfish Actions

Selfish actions do not consider the well being of others, and therefore they do not consider your own ultimate well being. When you cheat someone out of something s/he deserves, you eventually lose not only what you thought you would gain; you also lose what you would have gained if you had acted in a less selfish way. Every attempt to gain in a selfish manner eventually leads to loss and defeat, because selfish actions are not supported by the universal energy.

juLy 5

Aligned with Love

All complicated psychological states can be reduced to two simple ones: the state of being aligned with love and the state of being in the grip of fear.

Our greatest task is to find the compassionate Being within who loves and accepts us even when our fears are coming up. For that which holds our ego experience without judgment is aligned with love. When our fear is held gently and compassionately, it cannot be repressed or projected, so it has no power to hurt us or to hurt others.

july 6

Grace

Grace happens when you accept. Struggle happens when you reject or resist. Grace is natural. Struggle is unnatural. Grace is effortless. Struggle takes great effort. Struggle means that you get in the way. Grace means that you stay out of the way.

july 7

When Conditions are Right

When conditions are right for something to happen, it will happen without great effort. When conditions are not right, even great effort will not succeed.

july 8

Gratitude

Gratitude is the choice to see the love of God in all things. When you make this choice, you can no longer be miserable. For the choice to appreciate leads to happiness as surely as the choice to depreciate leads to unhappiness and despair.

One gesture supports and uplifts. The other devalues and tears down.

july 9

Strength and Flexibility

i f you want to understand what flexibility means, watch the behavior of a young sapling in the wind. Its trunk is thin and fragile, yet it has awesome strength and endurance. That is because it moves with the wind, not against it.

The tree is a symbol of strength and flexibility. You can develop the same strength of character by moving flexibly with all the situations in your life.

Stand tall and be rooted in the moment. Know your needs, but allow them to be met as life knows how. Do not insist that your needs be met in a certain way. If you do, you will offer unnecessary resistance. The trunk of the tree snaps when it tries to stand against the wind.

july 10

The White Flower

W e are the lotus floating on the murky surface of the pond. If you are looking for beauty without sadness, you will not find it. If you are looking for celebration without the poignancy of pain, you will search in vain. All that is transcendent comes from the lowly, the light from the dark, the white flower from the muddy waters of the pond.

july 11

There is no Map

Y ou cannot find a map that will take you to truth, nor can you rely on the experiences of others. If you ask one person which way you should go, he will say "go to the right." If you ask another person, he will say "go to the left."

Ask the pessimist where you can find truth and he will say "it was here yesterday. You missed it." Ask the optimist and he will reply: "it will be here tomorrow."

Who gives the correct answer? Is there, in fact, a correct answer? After you have been down a number of cul de sacs, you begin to realize that the answer that works for you may be different from the answer that works for others.

july 12

Divine Essence

W hen you are in touch with your Essence, you know that you are acceptable exactly as you are. There is nothing about you or anyone else that needs to be improved or fixed. To know your Essence, you must discard your self-judgments and your criticisms of your brother or sister.

july 13

Not knowing

i n our limited consciousness, we can't help thinking that we know what our experience means. However, the more we believe that we have the answers, the more our minds close to the mystery of our experience. Important insights and opportunities are missed because we are seeing our experience in a narrow or fixed way.

Today, practice not knowing what anything means. Just be with your experience without analyzing it or interpreting it.

Be neutral about your experience and that of others. Don't be for it or against it. Just accept it as it is and allow it to unfold.

july 14

Lifting the Veil

G od isn't in how life appears. That's just the veil. To see the truth, you must lift the veil.

God isn't the temporal, the changing, the inconstant, but the eternal, the unchanging, the constant. For human beings, love comes and goes. For God, love is constant.

If you are looking for God outside of you, you can live your whole life and never know that God exists. An about-face is necessary. You must turn within to the place where you are unconditionally aligned with Love.

When you are aligned with Love, you know that nothing else is real. You know that God is love and never stops being love.

july 15

Letting the Fire Burn Itself Out

You can be honest with the people you love without sharing every fearful thought or feeling that comes up. If you need to share every fear, you put others through an emotional buzz saw. That puts a big strain on your relationship.

If you are triggered by something someone else says, expressing your angry feelings may not be as helpful as riding them out until you understand what in you got triggered. Then, you can take more responsibility for your anger. You might even realize that your anger has very little to do with what the other person did or said.

Every relationship has its explosive moments. If you don't pour gasoline on the fire, the flames eventually die out. But if you insist on speaking to others when you are upset, don't be surprised if the fire escalates and begins to burn out of control.

july 16

Come to God with Empty Hands

The door to the Divine Presence opens when you no longer need to make reality fit your pictures of how it should be, when you can surrender everything you think you know and come to each moment empty of expectations.

When you are able to surrender in this way, you realize that God is not some abstraction, but a living presence in your life. It is the breath that animates all forms, the ultimate inclusive understanding, the quintessential blessing of love on all things.

july 17

Authenticity and Harmony with Others

Y ou come to harmony with others not through con-formity, but through authenticity. When you have the courage to be yourself, you find the highest truth you are capable of receiving. That truth is what enables you to reach across the aisle to your brother or sister.

You do not have to agree with others to value them and respect them. Because you accept your own uniqueness, you can honor the unique path that others take. Finding the truth in yourself, you recognize it when you see it manifest in others.

july 18

Freedom and Authority

i f you want to be free, you must have the courage to be yourself even when others judge you or disagree with you. And you must respect the right of others to be true to themselves, even when they push your buttons. You can't be free if you are allowing someone else to be an authority for you or if you are trying to be an authority figure for someone else.

july 19

The True Authority of Your Heart

true authority is rock-solid and self-nurtured. It does not need to gain the approval of others, nor does it desire to please self at the expense of others. It is not drawn outward into other people's dramas, nor inward into the attempt to satisfy personal wants and needs.

The true authority of your heart blesses you in your wholeness and it blesses others in theirs. It sees no lack in others or in self, so it does need to fix or be fixed, save or be saved. In this way, it skillfully avoids trespass.

july 20

Doing the Right Thing

Doing the right thing won't always win you friends and influence. Sometimes it results in being judged, ostracized, beaten, imprisoned, or worse.

Jesus did the right thing and he was crucified.

But the story of the crucifixion is not the story of God's punishment of us. It is the story of our punishment of each other and the attempt of our ego to kill the Spirit within us.

That attempt must necessarily be unsuccessful. That is what the resurrection means. You can kill the body, but you cannot kill the Spirit.

In the end, right outlives might. The voice of truth is heard as soon as fear subsides and the hearts of people open.

juLy 21

The Light Bearer

To pretend to be a light bearer before you have faced your own fear is to be an unhealed healer. It will be only a matter of time before you fall off your pedestal.

A bearer of the light does not deny the darkness. She embraces it. Her darkness. Everyone's darkness. She has the courage to walk through her fears, even when they seem overwhelming.

When there is nothing about you or anyone else that you are afraid to look at, the darkness has no more power over you. Then you can walk through the darkness and be the light.

juLy 22

Salvation is Now

Do not place salvation in the future or it will never come. Ask for it now. Accept it now.

When does Heaven come? When this moment is enough. When this place is enough. When this friend is enough. When these events and circumstances are acceptable. When you no longer crave something other than what stands before you.

juLy 23

What God Sees

he ego sees through a glass darkly. It sees the pain and suffering, but overlooks the potential for growth and transformation. It sees the crime, not the remorse and the opening to forgiveness. It sees the wound, not the healing into wholeness; the fall from grace, not the redemption; the crucifixion, not the resurrection.

God sees in a different way. Where the ego sees a problem or an obstacle, God sees an opportunity to love more deeply.

juLy 24

Miracles

iracles are rarely continuous with what has happened before. They interrupt that continuity.

They bring the unexpected. They challenge the dominant assumptions of consciousness.

They ask you to surrender your world view. They urge you to let go of your interpretation of life so that you can see the possibilities that lie beyond it.

july 25

Actions Speak Louder than Words

Your life is the fruit of your practice. What good are lovely sermons if the one who gives them does not practice what s/he preaches? Actions always speak louder than words. People emulate what you do, not what you say.

july 26

The Spark

Ignore the light within and it can barely be seen in the darkness. But attend to it and it grows into a steady flame. Feed that flame with acts of loving kindness and it becomes a blazing fire, a source of warmth and light for all who come close to it.

july 27

The Search for Answers

Remember that life does not come in a tidy package. It retains its ragged edges, its ambiguity, and alas, its mystery. That not necessarily a bad thing.

It is better for you to keep asking the questions than to find an answer that makes you dull and complacent.

juLy 28

Illusions

Illusions are born when you stop loving another person or yourself. The only way to dissolve illusions is to start loving right now in this moment.

juLy 29

God's Love

Even when we stray from the path, the power of God's love for us cannot be lost. It can be rejected, denied, hidden behind our guilt. But all rejection, denial, and secret guilt have limits.

Our connection to divine love can narrowed, covered up, or attenuated, but it can never be completely shut down. Beneath all our distortion and attempts to manipulate one another, God's love for us remains pure and untainted. It may be hard for us to access this love when we are trying to control, but when we are ready to let go and open our hearts, it is not difficult to reconnect with it.

july 30

The Source

Y ou keep looking for love from other people, not realizing that love comes only from your own consciousness. It has nothing to do with anyone else. Love comes from your willingness to think loving thoughts, experience loving feelings, and act in trusting, love-inspired ways

The source of love is within your own heart. Don't look to others to provide the love you need. Don't blame others for withholding their love from you. You don't need their love. You need your love.

july 31

A New Relationship Paradigm

t he only way to avoid co-dependent relationships is to befriend and honor the Self. Then you can build relationship on the truth of self-coherence. This is the new paradigm of relationship.

In the old relationship paradigm, the commitment to self is vitiated by the commitment to other. In seeking to please the other, self is abandoned. Since the abandoned self is incapable of love, this constitutes a vicious cycle of attraction and rejection.

All genuine relationship must be built on the foundation of your acceptance of and love for yourself. That is the primary spiritual gesture, the one that opens the door to real intimacy.

august 1

Love Takes No Hostages

One who loves without conditions places no limits on his freedom nor on anyone else's. He does not try to keep love, for to try to keep it is to lose it.

Love is a gift that must constantly be given as it is asked for in each moment. It takes no hostages, makes no bargains, and cannot be compromised by fear.

august 2

Stay in Your Own Life

Don't make decisions for other people. That will just take the focus away from your life. Let others find their own way. Support them. Encourage them. Cheer them on. But don't think you know what's good for them. You don't know.

When you take inappropriate responsibility for others, you overextend and weaken yourself. Don't do that. Stay in your own life and make your own decisions. Put your attention where it belongs. Listen to your guidance, honor it, act on it, and be committed to it. That is a full time job.

august 3

Acknowledging Your Fear

e ven if your fears are silly, you still need to acknowledge them. Saying "I'm scared" when you feel scared is being emotionally congruent. Pretending not to be scared when you are terrified is emotionally incongruent.

If you make friends with your fear, you may find that it subsides by itself. If not, then you need to keep acknowledging it and being gentle with yourself.

You can't force yourself not to be afraid. That strategy generally creates more fear.

august 4

Authentic Teachers

a uthentic spiritual teachers claim no authority over others, nor do they pretend to have the answers for other people. They do not preach. They do not try to fix. They simply accept people as they are and encourage them to find their own truth.

august 5

Setting Clear Boundaries

on't try to live through others or allow them to live through you. That will make the boundaries between you fuzzy and unclear. It will establish the conditions for co-dependence and mutual betrayal.

Set some limits and keep them clear. Sleep in your own bed. Prepare your own food. Clean up after yourself. Practice taking care of yourself and let others do the same for themselves.

You are not here to do for others what they must do for themselves. Nor are they here to live your life for you.

august 6

No One Else can Rescue You

our responsibility is to walk through your own pain. Even when you join your life with another's, this responsibility stays with you. Whenever you lose sight of it, or try to give it to someone else, you inevitably pay the price.

august 7

False Teachers

Do not seek the company of one who denies you the freedom to be yourself. Do not accept a teacher who tries to make decisions for you or to control your life.

Anyone who claims a special knowledge and sells it for a price is a false teacher. Anyone who asks you to give up your own ideas and experience and carry out his agenda is a false teacher. Anyone who asks for sexual favors in return for spiritual guidance is a false teacher. Anyone who encourages you to give away your power, your self-respect or your dignity is a false teacher.

You are responsible for the company you keep. Do not abide with such people.

august 8

The False Teachings of Fear and Guilt

Love is the cornerstone of all great spiritual teachings. Without love, there are just dogmas and rigid, fearful beliefs. Without love, there is no compassion or charity.

Those who judge others as sinful and seek to redeem them are just projecting their own fear and inadequacy. They use the words of religion as a substitute for the love they are unable to give or receive.

Do not judge these people, for they are in their own painful way crying out for love. But do not accept the guilt they would lay at your feet. It is not yours.

august 9

No Outcasts or Heathens

the ideas and behavior of certain people may challenge us and we may judge them and cast them out of our lives, but let us not think there is any justification for this. Our rejection of others is simply a result of our fear. There is nothing spiritual about it

If we believe in love and practice our faith, we must consider all men and women as equals, no matter how they look, how they act or what they believe. We can be sure that God loves and values the people we reject as much as S/he values us. For God, there are no outcasts or heathens.

august 10

Being with Our Pain

Sometimes by being with our pain in a compassionate way, we experience a shift. Sometimes we don't. However, we must give up the idea that our experience of pain means that we are bad and/or are being punished by God.

None of us are bad. We all make mistakes and we all need to forgive and be forgiven.

Sometimes pain is a messenger that brings us to the door. But nothing, not even the most profound pain, can force us to go through the door if we are not ready.

august 11

Hearing your Own Truth

Y ou alone know what course of action is best for the fulfillment of your purpose here. But that knowledge is sometimes buried deeply in your heart and it takes a lot of listening to connect with your inner wisdom and clarity. In some cases, hearing your own truth is not possible until you stop listening to what other people think you should do.

august 12

Be Gentle with Yourself

t oday, be gentle and patient with yourself. When you get up in the morning, be open to what the day has to teach you. When something difficult happens, remember that its primary purpose is to help you learn to love yourself and the other people who share your life.

When you go to bed at night, close your eyes and review your day. See those times when you experienced fear and understand how your unkindness toward others emanates from your inability to be patient and compassionate with yourself.

Forgive yourself for being harsh with yourself and affirm that you are willing to be more gentle. Know that it is a process. You cannot rush it or make it happen. But you can be willing and allow it to happen. You can learn to welcome peace in the midst of your fear.

august 13

Finding the Good

N o one is unworthy of love. Not you. Not your friends. Not even your enemies.

So stop condemning yourself and others. Be grateful for the love and nurturing that you have in your life. Focus on what is there, not on what is not there. Find the good in your life and you will reinforce it and extend it to others.

august 14

Repentance

i t is never too late for you repent from your unkind actions and make amends to those whom you have injured or judged unfairly. Your mistakes do not condemn you unless you insist on holding onto them.

Let them go. Stop punishing yourself. Stop punishing others. You can change. You can grow. You can be wiser than you were before. You can stop being a mouthpiece for fear and become a spokesperson for forgiveness and love.

No ship has ever been refused refuge in the harbor of forgiveness. No matter what you have said or done, you can still find the truth and come back on track. All you need to do is confess your mistakes and be willing to let them go.

august 15

Truth isn't Found in the Marketplace

i f you allow it, people will be only too glad to make you jump through hoops or stand in line in front of their concession stands. Give them the chance, and they will be only too glad to take your freedom away and give you the bill for their time.

Don't play by their rules. Don't be hoodwinked by the idea that there is something out there to achieve if only you had "more money" or were "more attractive, more spiritual, more intelligent" . . . you fill in the blank.

Don't line the pockets of those who make empty promises to you. It doesn't matter what they promise: more wisdom, more love, more abundance, more enlightenment, more peace of mind.

You already have more than any of these people can offer you. You just haven't claimed it yet.

august 16

Saying "No" in a Loving Way

y ou may not think that saying "no" can be a loving act. Yet, if your child puts his hand on a hot stove, you say "no" quickly and firmly. You do not want him to hurt himself. And then you put your arm around him and reassure him that you love him.

How many times does your brother come to you with his hand on the stove? You cannot support behavior that you know will be hurtful to another person. And you don't want your friends to support that kind of behavior in you.

august 17

Who is Responsible for Loving You?

Don't focus on how other people treat you. Focus on how you treat yourself. If you are in an abusive relationship, for example, don't focus on the abuser's behavior. Look instead at your own. Ask yourself if deciding to be with an abusive person is a nice way to treat yourself.

Be responsible for loving and taking care of yourself. Don't try to give this responsibility to anyone else.

Your assignment is a simple one. Love yourself right now! If you forget, just remember your assignment and start practicing. Tell yourself "I am responsible for loving myself in this moment. If I don't love myself, no one else will. The love of others can reach me only if I am loving myself."

If you are one-pointed in this practice, things will improve. You will stop betraying yourself. And when your self betrayal comes to an end, it will no longer be so easy for others to abuse or betray you.

august 18

Your Path

Your path has its own simple beauty and mystery. It is never what you think it is. Yet it is never beyond your ability to intuit the next step.

august 19

Standing for Truth in a Loving Way

Standing up for truth is a forceful act, but it should not be a violent one. There will be times when you must stand up for yourself and for others who are being mistreated. You cannot live your life in a state of fear, cowering in a corner while others make decisions for you. You must stand up and be counted. However, you can and should do this without attacking others.

It is important to stand up for the truth. However, if you don't stand in a loving way, it is not truth that you stand for.

august 20

God is Within

You prepare the inner temple for God to enter. And who is God but the One in you who knows and understands, the One who loves and accepts you without conditions, under all circumstances, now and for all time?

God is not outside of you, but in your heart of hearts. When you ask sincerely, this is the One who answers. When you knock, this is the One who opens the door.

august 21

The Call

D eeply imbedded in your psyche is the call to awaken. However, it does not sound like the call that anyone else hears. If you are listening primarily to others, don't be surprised if you don't hear the call when it comes.

august 23

Morality and Sex

C ontrary to what many people—including many clergy members —think and preach, there are only two kinds of sex that create suffering: non-consensual sex (rape or sex with a minor) and sex without love. Non-consensual sex is and should be a felony. Sex without love is unsatisfactory and addictive. More will always be needed. More sex, more partners, more stimulation. But more is never enough.

When you engage in non-consensual sex or sex without love, you dishonor yourself and the other person. This is true even if the person is your spouse. These types of discordant sexual activities fragment the energy of your union, destroy trust and exacerbate emotional wounds.

august 24

Using Affirmations to Deny Feelings

J esus said "Resist not Evil." If he were using today's lingo, he might say something like "what you resist, persists."

If you are angry at someone and you try to replace your angry thoughts with loving thoughts, one of two things will happen. Either you will be successful at repressing the anger (a form of denial) so that it continues to exist in your psyche even though you pretend that it isn't there. Or you won't be successful.

Actually, here it's advantageous not to succeed, because then you will have to deal with the anger, acknowledge it, find out what triggered it, etc. Anger is not transformed through denial, but through understanding.

Unfortunately, much of the so called "new age" teaching encourages us to hide our negative thoughts/emotions behind a wall of denial and wallpaper over them with positive ones. But then, at the first major sign of stress, the wallpaper comes peeling off the wall.

There are two ways that you can deal with fear.

1. Deny your fear and pretend that you are not afraid.

2. Admit that you are afraid and face your fear.

The first way takes you round and around in circles of avoidance and projection. The second way leads you to face to face with yourself.

august 22

The Body

The body is not bad or inferior in any way. It is simply temporal. You will never find ultimate meaning by satisfying its needs. Nor might I add will you find ultimate meaning by denying its needs.

Taking care of the body is an act of grace. Preoccupation with bodily pleasures or pains is anything but graceful.

august 25

Guarantees

When love is present, you don't worry about the future. Only when love is lacking do you insist on guarantees.

august 26

Fear of Sex

Lovemaking can and should be a joyful act, an act of surrender to the divine in yourself and your partner. Physical love is no less beautiful than other forms of love, nor can it be separated from them. If you view physical love as unholy, you will probably experience it that way, not because it is, but because you perceive it that way.

august 27

Emotional and Sexual Betrayal

When love is mutual and you and your partner are surrendered to each other emotionally, sex is uplifting and sacred. But when communication in your relationship becomes careless and shoddy, when time is not taken for one-to-one intimacy, your relationship becomes a shell in which you both hide. Energy and commitment disappear from your union. And sex becomes an act of physical betrayal.

It is not surprising then that you and/or your partner look outside the relationship for satisfaction. Infidelity is a symptom of your emotional and physical disconnection from your partner. Unfortunately, it involves another person in the dynamics and makes it more difficult for healing and reconciliation to take place.

august 28

Love is the Ascending Force

When you act in a loving way and speak loving words, the Spirit dwells in you and is awakened in others. At such times, physical reality does not seem as dense as it seemed before.

When love is present, the body and the world are infused with light, possibility and celebration of goodness. The world you see when love is present in your heart is not the same world that you see when you are preoccupied with your ego needs.

august 29

Serving Others

You cannot serve others if you are attached to what you offer or how others receive it. You must get out of the way so that Spirit can work through you.

Service is an opportunity to love, not a job description. You cannot serve and have an identity or an agenda.

When you help someone else, you help yourself. You help your mother and father. You help your third cousin. You help the drunk on the street corner.

Your help goes where it is needed. You will never know all the people who are touched by your loving actions, nor do you need to know.

august 30

Abundance and Bliss

You experience scarcity and sadness only when you find fault with the situation you are presented with in the moment. When you see the situation and feel gratitude for it, you experience only abundance and bliss.

august 31

Healing the Healer

the compulsion to heal others can be a major obstacle to your own healing. It can even hurt others, however unintentionally.

No one can be a full time healer. It is too much to ask from any human being. Every healer needs to take time off to re-center and re-charge.

Even those who are capable of great love must be willing to look at their own fear when it comes up or they will project it onto others.

A healer's first commitment must be to do no harm to others. That means she must be vigilant about her own abilities and intentions. Only when she knows she is intact, can she offer to help others.

Healers often have martyr complexes. They feel responsible for healing everyone and when people don't heal, they feel it is their fault. They carry the cross even when it is not necessary.

It will never be possible for you to cure all of the suffering you see in the world. Trying to do so will only undermine your ability to serve the people you are able to help. So put your cross down and take some time to meet your own emotional and spiritual needs. Nurture and heal yourself so that you can re-charge and be in a position to help others.

september 1

The Present Moment

Happiness happens only in the present moment. If you become concerned about whether you will be happy tomorrow or even five minutes from now, you won't be able to be happy now.

All of the chaos and confusion in your mind can be transcended through your simple decision to be wholly present and attentive right now. That is the miraculous truth.

september 2

Walking the Tightrope

We always have two voices in our heads. The voice of the past says "Don't open. It's too scary. Don't you remember what happened when...?" The voice of the future says "This is taking so long, why don't you just jump in and do it?" The past tries to hold us back and the future tries to rush us.

Like it or not, you need to listen to both voices and reassure them that they have been heard. Then, you can rebalance and come back to center. Then, you can find a pace that feels good for right now.

That is what the tightrope walker must do. She can't worry about losing her balance in the past. She can't dream about a perfect performance in the future. She needs to focus on what's happening right now. She needs to put one foot in front of the other.

Every step is an act of balance. Every step is a spiritual act.

septembeR 3

Completing the Past

there are no past lives, any more than there are past experiences. The belief in the past is what limits your ability to be fully present in the moment.

Do not go in search of memories from the past. If they come up, acknowledge them, be with them and integrate them. Do this not to empower the past, but to complete it, so that you can be present now. Anything that takes you away from your immediate communion with life is not helpful.

septembeR 4

Clearing the Air

do not go to sleep angry with the people you love. Do not let the sun rise or set without making peace. Nurture your relationships. Be ready to let go of thoughts and feelings that can only injure and separate.

Negative thoughts and feeling states must be cleared on no less than a daily basis. So find ways to soften and come together when you feel angry or hurt. Find a way to admit that you went into fear. Find a way to surrender your need to be right and to make the other person wrong.

You are both right in your desire to be loved and respected. You are both wrong in your attempt to blame the other person for your unhappiness.

september 5

Finding Inner Authority

The more unstable life seems, the more we gravitate toward the "security" promised by authority figures. We marry authority figures, elect them, go to their churches and join their cults. In time, many of these people are unmasked and discredited and we learn to take our power back and pick up the pieces of our lives.

When we uproot ourselves to follow the empty promises of charismatic leaders, we tend to get beaten up by our experiences. Then, we return humbled, shovels in hand, and begin the work of planting.

Those who abandon their roots will learn to find them. Those who have sought authority in other people will learn to find it in themselves.

september 6

The Dance of Acceptance

acceptance is a life-long dance. You get better at it the more you do it. But you never dance perfectly.

Sometimes you get tired and you proclaim "I shall dance no more." But then, unexpectedly, you fall in love, or someone makes you a business offer you can't refuse. No matter how hard you try, or how much you complain, you can't stop the dance.

Mistakes are part of the dance. But some people don't know this. Their business fails or their partner leaves them and they blow their brains out. They play for very high stakes.

Sometimes we take the dance a little too seriously. We forget that we are here to learn.

We need to lighten up, stand back, and take some small pleasure in the dance itself. If we don't learn to laugh at ourselves from time to time, our journey becomes heavy and oppressive.

The more unhappy you are, the harder the dance becomes, because you must dance with your unhappiness. That's why acceptance is so important. The more you accept life as it unfolds, the easier the dance becomes.

september 7

Facilitating Healing

Y ou cannot help people heal unless you are feeling love in your heart. Then what you say and do will flow through your love, not through your fear, and you will inspire, encourage and uplift.

Remember, you are here to empower others, not to fix them or to take responsibility for their pain. So don't force your gift on others. Give to those who ask for your help and are ready to receive it. Then, you will not trespass on them or exhaust your own energies.

september 8

Trust

W hen you know that your life is okay, no matter how ragged and unfinished it seems, there is room for movement. A shift can happen. A door can open.

The most important door is the one to your heart. If it is open, then the whole universe abides in you. If it is closed, then you stand alone against the world.

september 9

Blaming Yourself

It isn't helpful to obsess about your mistakes. Guilt is productive only when it helps you learn from your mistakes so that you can act more responsibly in the future.

If there is nothing you can do to make the situation better, then just accept it as it is. Sometimes, there's nothing to be done. Blaming yourself or others isn't helpful.

You aren't the only one who has strayed from the path or put your foot in your mouth. Hopefully, in time, you will be able to laugh at your mistakes and put them behind you.

september 10

Centering

Centering means staying with what you know and dropping what you don't know. You don't know that the past is going to repeat itself. It may or it may not.

Old patterns may dissolve or they may reappear. You don't know these things. All you know is how you feel about what's happening right now.

If you can stay with this, then you can be honest with yourself and with others about your experience. You can say what you are able to commit to and what you cannot commit to right now.

Things may change in the future, but you can't live right now hoping they are going to change. You must be where you are, not where you want to be.

september 11

Attachment to your Story

You are free to be responsible for your life right now, but do you want to be? Are you ready to give up your attachment to your story?

The problems you perceive in your life are projections of the internal conflict: "I want but I cannot have." If you would allow yourself to have what you want, or if you would stop wanting it because you know you can't have it, this conflict would cease.

Your story of "seek but do not find" would be over. But are you ready to give up the drama? Has your pain, your scarcity, your need to fix or be fixed become part of your personality? Has your story become your identity?

Letting your drama go means letting the past dissolve right here, right now. That means that you are totally responsible for what you choose. There are no more excuses.

september 12

Emptying the Cup

When you are attached to what you have, how can you bring in anything new in? To bring in something new, something fresh, something unpredictable, you must surrender something old, stale and habitual.

If you want the creative to manifest within you, you must surrender all that is not creative. Then in the space made by that surrender, creativity rushes in.

If the cup is full of old, cold tea, you cannot pour new, hot tea into it. First you have to empty the cup. Then you can fill it.

september 13

Release from Prison

i f you are getting three hot meals and a bed to sleep in, you don't want to talk about freedom. It doesn't matter that someone else plans your day: tells you when to eat, when to exercise and when to go to sleep. It doesn't matter that the door to your room is locked every night.

The idea of living without these amenities is frightening to you. You don't know how you would survive outside your cell. But consider this: one day the guard is going to come and unlock the door and tell you it's time to leave. And you will have to leave, whether you want to or not. Even if you get down on your knees and beg to stay, you will be forced to leave.

Under these circumstances, there is only one question you must ask and it's not "what time is breakfast served?" It is "Are you ready for that day and, if not, why not?"

september 14

Stopping

W hen it is clear that something isn't working, stop doing it. Stop putting your energy into it. Step back and away from it. Detach. Let go. If you don't stop, you will make the situation worse than it is.

september 15

Waiting for Direction

*t*he best results occur when we stop trying to force things to be the way we think they should be. When we try to force a solution to a problem, we often overcompensate and create a new problem.

Sometimes it is better to just stop doing what we know is not working and take some time to re-center and reconnect with the core truth within us. Then the course of action we set will be more organic, congruent, and meaningful.

We all need time to breathe and to be. It's a sacred time. It's a time when we gather our power and our direction. If we don't take this time, we may act prematurely or impulsively. Our actions may lack power or they may result in unfortunate consequences we did not anticipate.

september 16

To Forgive is to Undo

*t*o forgive is not to do, but to undo. To undo a judgment, say to yourself "The judgment I made is untrue. It was made in ignorance. It says more about me than it does about you. But it is not even true about me. This judgment is a reflection of my fear. I would rather face my fear directly than to judge you or myself."

september 17

Walking through Closed Doors

even if you don't know why a door is closed, at least respect the fact that it is closed and don't struggle with the doorknob. If the door was open, you would know it. Wanting it to be open does not make it open.

Much of the pain in your life happens when you attempt to walk through closed doors or try to put square pegs into round holes. You try to hold onto someone who is ready to go, or you try to get somebody to do something before s/he is ready. Instead of accepting what is and working with it, you interfere with it and try to manipulate it to meet your perceived needs. Obviously, this doesn't work. It just creates strife for yourself and others.

september 18

Living Alone

Living alone is a requirement for living successfully with another person. If you haven't lived alone, you haven't had time to find out who you are and what you need in a relationship. Chances are you have lived trying to please parents, teachers, friends and lovers. In order to gain the acceptance and approval of these significant others, you may have neglected your own needs and desires.

Going from one relationship into another is not going to help you get rooted in your own experience. You need to take some time to establish your own rhythms and find out what's really important to you.

septemBeR 19

Changing Commitment

When someone ceases to be committed to a relationship, a shift takes place. Energy is withdrawn from one direction and placed in a new direction.

You can argue until you are blue in the face about whether it is right or wrong that someone's commitment changes, but it won't do you any good. You cannot prevent other people from going forward in their growth, even if you don't agree with their decisions.

If you look deeply enough, you will see that every apparent "loss" you experience brings an unexpected gain. When one person leaves a relationship that is not growing into deeper intimacy, the other person is set free too.

september 20

Letting Go

When something in your life is not working, you try to fix it. Then, if that doesn't work, you may pretend for a while that it's fixed even though you know it isn't. Finally, you realize that your heart just isn't in the job or the relationship. That's when you are ready to let go of it.

Letting go is an act of substantial courage. There is always some degree of pain in the release of someone or something that once brought you joy and happiness. You will have to be patient and mourn the loss. But when your mourning is over, you will see things differently.

As the old dies, the new is born. The phoenix rises from the ashes of destruction. If you stay centered in your life while the fire burns around you, opportunities you never could have dreamed of will come into your life.

september 21

The Rewards of Partnership

as long as there is growth and honesty in your relationship, it is worthy of your commitment.

That doesn't mean that it's perfect. Even in the best relationships, doubts and fears continue to arise for both people. However, mature couples learn to hold those doubts and fears with compassion. They learn to be patient with and accepting of each other.

In time, the hard shell around your hearts begins to crack open. Where fear used to hold you back, you learn to take baby steps forward. You learn to walk through your fears and stretch your hand out to your partner. You learn to heal together and to trust each other.

And then you experience a gentleness born of the struggle, a sweetness born of the pain. Then there is a twinkle in your eyes when you look at your partner. It isn't the same twinkle that was there when you first met.

It is a different one. It tells of your journey through fear and projection into the heart of acceptance and love.

september 22

The Fruit of your Labor

on't have unrealistic expectations of how or when your needs will be met. If you ask for an apple, and an apple comes back, it doesn't mean that you are God's favorite child. It just means that it's apple season. Be happy. Celebrate your good fortune.

If you ask for an apple, and you get a banana, you can have two attitudes. One is: "At least it's a fruit!" The other is: "God doesn't like me because he sent me a banana and I hate bananas."

If you want something bad enough, getting a banana won't stop you. But most of us don't know that. Nine out of ten times we throw the banana back and then slip on the peel!

Remember, if it's banana season and you need an apple, you might have to be patient and wait for apple season! Are you willing to wait? How much do you really want an apple?

You see, this is completely about you. It has nothing to do with anyone else!

september 23

Addicted to Romance

I t is easy to get addicted to romance. Like all of us, you enjoy the emotional highs of being in love. So, when one relationship ends and you feel sad and low, you immediately look for another relationship to cheer you up.

Falling in love is truly like a drug. It makes you very high for a short period of time, but inevitably you crash. Then, if you are an addict, you go out and get another fix. You find someone else to fall in love with and you lose yourself in each other.

You don't have to have that much in common to fall in love. When you are high, it seems as if you could share anything with your partner. It's only when the drug wears off that you realize that you and this other person may not have much in common. It can be very painful to look at someone whose bed you have been sharing for three or four months and realize that you have very different values, interests, and goals in life.

Everyone likes falling in love. Who wouldn't like a hormone rush? But very few people realize how dangerous it can be. Indeed, very few couples survive falling in love. The ones who do survive are the ones who either took the time to get to know each other before they fell in love or the ones who were just plain lucky.

september 24

Accepting Differences

i n any relationship there will be times when you do not agree with your partner. The question is: how well do you handle your disagreements? Is there room in your relationship for both of you to have differing opinions, as well as interests and activities that you don't share?

A relationship that requires total agreement and sharing to thrive is an unrealistic one. That is far too much to expect from any relationship.

When your love for your partner is based on acceptance, not on agreement, you have a better chance of creating real intimacy. Contrary to what many believe, a good relationship does not require that you share everything with your partner. Rather, it requires that you establish a mutual trust with your partner that allows you to be authentic and express yourselves, separately and together.

To be sure, intimacy comes from the intensity and consistency of your embrace. But it also comes from your willingness to let go and support each other when there are things that you cannot share.

september 25

Heartfelt Communication

Heartfelt communication requires honesty on the part of the speaker and acceptance on the part of the listener. When the speaker is blaming and the listener is judging, you don't have communication; you have attack.

To communicate effectively you must do the following:

1. Listen to your thoughts and feelings until you know what they are and understand that they belong only to you.

2. Honestly express how you think and feel to others without blaming them or trying to make them responsible for what you are thinking or how you are feeling.

3. Listen without judgment to any thoughts and feelings others want to convey to you. Remember, what they say, think, and feel describes their state of consciousness. It may or may not have anything to do with your own.

If you find that you need to fix other people or defend yourself when other people express their thoughts and feelings to you, you probably aren't listening and it is very likely that your buttons are being pushed. They may be mirroring some part of you which you may not want to look at.

september 26

Communication is a Bridge

When you are blaming and judging others in your life, you will experience separation. You can bridge this separation only by communicating with others in a non-hostile way. If you are feeling anger, for example, let the other person know that you are angry, but don't blame him or her for "making" you angry. Don't hide your anger or disguise it. Acknowledge it openly. Take responsibility for it.

Communicate what you feel honestly and then listen without judgment to how others feel. That way you avoid the extremes of stuffing your feelings or projecting them and attacking others.

september 27

Unmasking Truth

All judgments, opinions, interpretations disguise the truth. They are all forms of trespass.

As long as you are judging someone, you cannot see the truth about that person. What you see is just a mask.

Only when you take your own mask off can you see behind the masks others wear. That's when you see who people really are. That is when you see others as God sees you.

september 28

Giving Advice

When other people ask for your opinion or advice, please share your experience with the caveat that it might not apply to them. Sharing what works for you can be helpful to others if you hold the space for them to hear their own guidance.

When we feel a compulsion to share, the desire to help others can be an attack in disguise. So we do have to be vigilant and ask ourselves "Can I share this respectfully without being attached to how it is received?' and "Will my story be likely to empower the other person?' If the answer is "no", then it is best to defer.

Just because someone asks for your advice doesn't mean that you have any helpful advice to give. If the truth is that you don't know what to say, then saying "I don't know" can be a great gift to the other person, because it helps him/her turn inward to find the answer.

september 29

Demons Rising Up

Some conflicts between people have little to do with the specifics of a situation and a lot to do with the inner demons that are disturbed and brought out of their dark depths into the light of conscious awareness.

Your partner is not responsible for your demons, nor are you responsible for his or hers. But you are midwives to each other's growth into greater awareness. Living with another person often pushes your deepest buttons and sets off unexpected explosions. Your fears simply cannot stay hidden. It isn't always pleasant business.

If you expect it to be pleasant all of the time then you will be sadly disappointed. Every relationship moves from romance to realism to the depths of despair. Couples fall from grace just as individuals do. Each has a dark night of the soul, a grappling with the demonic realm.

Couples who face their demons and walk through their fears win a decisive battle against their own ignorance. They are the ones who transcend the limits they have previously placed on love. They are the ones who learn how to love without conditions.

september 30

Refraining from Projection

N othing derails a relationship faster than frequent excursions into guilt and blame.

Don't forget the discipline you must bring to your own life. You are not always happy. When you live alone, you have moments of sadness, self-judgment, fear, anxiety; you have feelings of unworthiness and failure. You need to ride out these moments and hold these thoughts and feelings compassionately or you cannot function in life.

What makes you think that you won't have to do the same thing when you are in a relationship? The truth is you need to be even more compassionate with yourself and responsible for your thoughts and feelings when you live with someone else. That is because your egoic tendency and that of your partner will be to blame each other for your negative emotional states. To refrain from this kind of projection is one of the greatest challenges of relationship.

OCTOBER 1

Holding the Space for Another

When your friend or partner is sad or angry, you need to know that those feelings are his/her responsibility, not yours. You may have triggered the feelings, but you are not their ultimate cause, nor are you responsible for changing how the other person feels.

That doesn't mean that you cease to care. You can care deeply without taking on a responsibility that does not belong to you. Because you don't buy into inappropriate guilt here, you remain emotionally free to respond to the other person in a loving way.

You can give this person a great gift just by listening to what s/he is feeling without trying to change or fix anything. You would not be able to do this if you felt responsible for this person's pain or sadness. Because you don't feel responsible, you can hold the space for the other person to come to terms with his or her emotions. This simple gesture of support can have a very profound result. It lets the person know that s/he is loved and accepted regardless of what s/he is feeling. Thus, it strengthens the friendship at the most fundamental level.

october 2

Relationship as a Spiritual Path

One of the paradoxes of relationship is that we give our power away to others in order to learn to honor ourselves more completely. We become co-dependent with others in order to learn how to have better boundaries. We blame others so that we can learn to take responsibility for our own mistakes.

It is all a set-up. We look for love and happiness through other people only to learn that we can find love and happiness only in our own hearts and minds.

Being in a relationship helps us learn to stand alone. It helps us gain confidence being ourselves and expressing who we are. The "We" is an incubator for the "I," or true Self, in each person. And when the true Self is actualized by both people, the spiritual purpose of the partnership is fulfilled.

october 3

Exploring Heaven and Hell

Your relationship will take you to the heights of heaven and the depths of hell. Both angels and devils live in your embrace and move with you in your journey toward self-forgiveness.

If you expect your relationship to be only happy and inspiring, how will you deal with the times when you feel repelled by or disconnected from your partner? How will you deal with your sadness, your doubts and fears when they come up?

No relationship, no matter how well suited the partners are to one another, no matter how much they love each other, is going to be free of struggle and turmoil. In any relationship, there are inevitable ups and downs, moments of connection and disconnection.

How you hold the moments of disconnection is as important as how you celebrate the moments of connection. Can you hold your pain and your partner's pain compassionately or do you deny it and try to make it go away?

Are you facing you fear, your anger and your anxiety or are you projecting them onto your partner? Do you use the challenges of the relationship to look more deeply at yourself, or do you run away and hide or threaten to leave the relationship every time there are misunderstandings?

Are you bringing your darkness to the light and learning to love it? Or are you hiding your shadowy material in some inaccessible psychic cave where others cannot see it? Are you moving toward pretense and denial or toward greater honesty and transparency?

OCtOBeR 4

Asking for Help

m any couples seek help only when mutual trust has been destroyed and it is too late to put the pieces back together. Don't wait until your relationship falls apart to seek help. Recognize when you are unable to forgive each other and rebound emotionally from your mutual trespasses. If you see that you are losing your emotional resilience and are frequently blaming each other for the problems that arise, it is time to ask for help. There is nothing weak or cowardly about asking for help when it is needed. On the contrary, it is a gesture of mutual courage, strength and caring about your relationship.

OCtOBeR 5

Are you at Peace?

W hen you are firmly committed to your inner journey, where you go outwardly becomes irrelevant. The real journey is the journey to peace within your own heart.

The only question that can be asked on the inward journey is "are you at peace?" If you are not at peace, then you have identified with something outside of yourself.

Peace is always there. It seems to disappear only because you turn your attention elsewhere.

october 6

The Road to Nowhere

there is a road going by, but you don't know where it is going. You don't know whether to go right or left, or whether to stay where you are. You don't know.

Sooner or later, out of boredom no doubt, you will make a choice. You will go right or left. And you will get excited thinking that you have made the right decision until you come to difficult terrain, and then you will be convinced that you went the wrong way. This will happen whether you go right or left. It makes no difference.

On the Road to Nowhere, it does not matter which way you go, because the road is circular and eventually returns to the same place. On the Road to Nowhere, the question is not "where are you going?" because you aren't going anywhere in particular. The question is "How are you going? Are you enjoying the journey?"

When you are going somewhere, the goal is very important. But when you aren't going anywhere, the goal is meaningless. The only thing that is important then is your state of consciousness. Are you going happily or sadly? Are you blessing those you pass along the way or cursing them?

octobeR 7

Self Betrayal

Who is responsible for the fact that you choose to be with people who betray you? Are they responsible or are you?

When you trust people who do not deserve your trust, you get hurt. And then, instead of seeing your error and learning from it, you tend to blame the person who betrayed you, which shifts the responsibility inappropriately.

And when that doesn't work, you might try to beat yourself up by engaging in some kind of self-destructive behavior like picking up a bottle, overeating or having promiscuous sex. That way you get to punish yourself without taking responsibility for your role in what happened.

Better to take responsibility for the decisions that you make and leave the self-crucifixion out. If you have a pattern of attracting people who treat you unfairly, then be more careful about whom you trust. Let people win your trust over time. Don't give your power away to others just because you want their love and approval.

Don't depend on others to give you the love, the approval, or the safety you need to give to yourself. Give it to yourself and then you cannot be betrayed.

october 8

Truth and Paradox

truth is paradoxical. To grasp the whole of it, you must approach it from all sides. One sided approaches lead only to partial truths.

Until you concede the paradoxical nature of truth, you will not transcend conflict in consciousness or relationship. Only when you concede the validity of all points of view can you move out of duality.

october 9

Conflict or Ambivalence

to push for a decision in the face of conflict or ambivalence is a way of punishing yourself or others. Don't try to force a decision when you aren't ready to make one. Instead, embrace both sides of the conflict. Acknowledge all the things you want about the job or the relationship and all of the things that make you want to run away. Get your psychic arms around all of it.

Stop holding your breath and breathe deeply. Take the pressure off. Being with conflict and ambivalence in a compassionate way brings a peaceful acceptance, from which clarity springs when it is time.

october 10

Peace in the midst of Conflict

To be peaceful in the midst of conflict, you must create respect for everyone's ideas and experiences. And you must also create a deep level of emotional and physical safety so that people know that they won't be attacked or ostracized for expressing themselves honestly.

When people are committed to love and equality, disagreements do not result in separation, but in dialogue and increased understanding.

october 11

Softening the Sword's Edge

As long as you are trying to choose between two strongly held points of view you will sharpen the edge between them. The pressure to decide is a double edged sword. It hurts everyone it touches.

Step away from the pressure and the urgency. Be patient with yourself. Get your arms around your entire experience. Take the sword of division and love it. Love it until its edge softens. Love it so that it can no longer do harm to yourself or others. Turn that sword into a ploughshare.

Then you can decide. Because then you will rest in the place of acceptance where judgments dissolve and love is born.

OCTOBER 12

To Choose or Not to Choose

When you make a choice wholeheartedly and do the very best you can, you don't experience much conflict. Even if it turns out that it was the wrong choice, you learn from it and move on.

If you can't choose wholeheartedly, the best thing that you can do is embrace your ambivalence and stop putting pressure on yourself to decide. Be patient with yourself and learn to accept all of the voices within your psyche. You don't have to act on any of these voices. Just listen to them and see what they need to say to you.

If you make your ambivalence okay, it will move when its ready to move. Direction will come when it's time.

You can't force yourself to choose before you are ready. If you do, you will probably have regrets.

OCTOBER 13

Seeing the Whole Elephant

You don't see all of the truth. You see just a piece of it. When you look at an elephant, you see only the tail and when your friend looks s/he sees only the trunk. No matter how hard you try you cannot understand the meaning of "trunk, "nor can your friend understand the meaning of "tail." Only one who sees the whole elephant understands both trunk and tail and the relationship between them.

octoBeR 14

Both Sides of the Coin

i n relationships, as in consciousness, both sides of the coin must be accepted as equal. Once cannot move out of conflict with another until the experience of both people has been honored.

Agreement is never the issue, although it seems to be. The issue is always: can we honor each other's experience?

octoBeR 15

Taking the Hook Out of Your Mouth

t here are only two things you or anyone else needs to understand. First, you need to understand that your experience is perfect for you. There is nothing about you or your experience that needs to be changed or fixed.

The other thing you need to understand is that the experience of other people is perfect the way it is. Like you, they do not need to be reformed, educated or fixed.

Remember these two things and you will create less suffering in your life. You will stop judging, blaming or crucifying yourself or at least become aware of your self-judgments and work on forgiving them. And you will stop judging, blaming, crucifying other people or at least become aware of your judgments about others and see that they point to parts of your own consciousness that are crying out for acceptance and healing.

This not only lets others off the hook. It also helps you take the hook out of your own mouth.

OCTOBER 16

Beyond Words

Reading a lot of words is exhausting. We do not need a lot of words. The more words we have, the more we argue about what they mean. And the more we argue, the less we understand.

Good teachers give us only a few words and then leave us to digest them. For example, Jesus told us "love your enemies." He also showed us how to do what he asked of us. Do we really need to add anything to this teaching to make it more clear?

OCTOBER 17

Clairvoyance

Spiritual powers are helpful only when they are used in a responsible way. If you find you have spiritual powers, you must be very careful to stay centered in your love for yourself and others. If you don't, you will be seeing through the lens of your own fear and you will give your power away to what you see.

Since no one is aligned with love at all times, remember that everything that you see will not be accurate or helpful, so you need to discriminate. Separate the wheat from the chaff.

In Corinthians it is said: "First they saw through a glass darkly and then face to face." To see "face to face" is to see things as they are without distortion, without interpretation. That is what true clairvoyance is.

When you can see without prejudice, predisposition or fear, then the lens will be clear. Until then, you will be seeing through a cloudy lens.

octoBeR 18

Unity in Diversity

When we look for agreement in the world we live in, we find factionalism and conflict. Only when we stop looking for agreement and start accepting our differences and creating a safe place to express them do we experience the core equality that unites us as human beings.

octoBeR 19

The Answers are Simple

You can spend your whole life chasing complicated solutions to your problems, but it will be a waste of time. The answers are simple. And they are close at hand.

Nobody else can make you happy or sad, nor can you make anyone else happy or sad. Your happiness or sadness belongs only to you and theirs belongs to them.

Don't waste your time blaming someone else for your mistakes or accepting guilt for the mistakes others make. Be responsible for what you think, say or do. Let others be responsible for what they think, say or do..

Keep these simple truths in front of you at all times and act accordingly. The way is straight. It appears to be crooked only when you try to twist it to accommodate your fear or your guilt.

OCTOBER 20

You were not Elected Savior

You do not ask others to do what you can do for your-self. You do not give your power away to others. Why should others give their power or responsibility to you?

Do what you can do for others. Give help when it is asked for and you can give it freely. But do not do for others what they must learn to do for themselves. If you insist on taking false responsibility for others, you invite their blame when what you do is not to their liking.

You were not elected as a savior. So please don't try to be one.

OCTOBER 21

Stepping Beyond Fear

If you want to go beyond your fear, you must first go through it. You must learn to be in fear without beating yourself up, without projecting your anxieties onto others. You must learn to walk with fear as your companion so that you get to know it. If you don't take the time to discover what your fear is all about, you will not be able to step beyond it.

oCtoBeR 22

Empowering Others

even if you can do the task better than your brother can, you must let him do it. Whatever he has chosen belongs to him. Stand back and make room for him. Don't even look over his shoulder.

If you want to teach, let your students watch while you demonstrate what needs to be done. Then let them practice by themselves. When they have learned what you can teach them, send them on their way.

Do not foster dependency in others. When the student keeps coming back for more instruction, you know a dependent pattern is there. Do not encourage it, even if it benefits you financially.

A good teacher empowers the student. A good therapist helps her client learn the skills she needs to make it on her own.

oCtoBeR 23

To Love is to be in the Heart

to love is to be in the heart. You cannot love from any other place. When you are in your heart, you feel not only your own pain, but the pain of everyone you meet. That is what it means to feel compassion.

Love is not a magic potion. It is not the raging of hormones. It has very little to do with sexuality, although sexuality can be an expression of love. It is about letting others into your heart.

october 24

Perfection

Perfection is never found in the object. It is found in the attitude of the one who looks. When the lens through which you look is clear, all objects seen through that lens are beautiful.

october 25

Expansion of Consciousness

When new energy comes into your life, your consciousness expands and is no longer comfortable working within the old limits you once accepted. Old forms of expression dissolve or crack and new, more spacious forms must be found.

The more you grow in consciousness, the more you move through various forms. It can be a little disorienting. It can feel a little unsafe.

That is why it is so important that you learn to create a safe, nurturing space for yourself where you can be quiet, assimilate and ground the new energy. It gives you time to inhabit the new form before you try to express yourself through it.

New energy sends you out on a limb. You see things there you have never seen before. But then you have to climb back down and find your roots again. Unless you take the time to get grounded, you may find that you get overextended, lose your balance and fall to the ground.

october 26

Control of Others

L ove lifts you up and inspires you. It can be the greatest blessing. Yet as soon as you love someone your ego goes crazy
and tries to take control.

Love brings everything shadowy up to the surface so it can
be witnessed and transformed. You are either willing to look
or you aren't.

Love gives you homework to do. It asks you to become aware
of your fears and insecurities so that you don't project them onto
the person you care about. That is the quickest way to destroy a
relationship.

Don't turn the blessing of love into a curse. Acknowledge your
fears to your partner and ask for help in walking through them.

october 27

Dying into Truth

t ruth cannot be described in words or concepts. Don't be
seduced by elaborate images or nice sounding words. They
place an unnecessary obstacle between you and the Supreme
Reality.

When you enter truth, your need to intellectualize or romanticize your experience begins to dissolve. Your ego has a hard
time getting a foothold.

But ego is not beaten down or destroyed. It dies into truth.
It yields to something deeper and more profound. It is not a
painful act, but an ecstatic one.

OCTOBER 28

Everywhere and Nowhere

Nowhere is not a bad place. It's just the place you come to when you no longer have "somewhere else" to go. It's just the place you come to when you stop avoiding this moment. It is just the place you inhabit when you realize that the journey doesn't have to do with anyone but you.

You are the subject: your thoughts, your feelings, your words, and your actions. If you are willing to turn your attention to these, then you don't have to run around like Don Quixote fighting windmills and saving damsels in distress. You can be where you are and address the origin of joy and suffering inside yourself.

Enlightenment doesn't involve getting something you do not have. It involves relinquishing a barrier you have placed between yourself and truth. It is not so much a finding of truth, but a giving up of illusion.

OCTOBER 29

The Power of Belief

The stronger our beliefs are, the more we manifest in alignment with them. As we believe, so do we think, act and react. We create our life based on what we believe, regardless of how true or erroneous our beliefs may be.

october 30

Ending the Pain of Separation

When you know that the spiritual journey is not an external one, you stop losing yourself in the world. You see that the world is not causing your suffering. You are causing it.

So you look at yourself. You understand that suffering cannot be ended in the world until it is ended in your heart. It cannot be ended in your brother or sister until it is ended in you.

Authentic spirituality is the path to your own heart. It leads through all your fears and self-deceptions. It is not a journey of escape. It is a journey through your pain to end the pain of separation

october 31

Now is the only Time there is

Every moment contains all other moments. This moment contains all the past and all the future.

That is why the central teaching of all spiritual traditions is to claim our awareness in this moment. While this moment may be only one point on the circle, any point will do. Any point is the alpha and omega.

A special time or place is not needed. Here is as good a place as any; now is as good a time as any. There is nothing that you have to do first. There is nothing you have to do later. There is only what is happening now. That is your only responsibility.

NOVEMBER 1

The Dance of Being

Your job is not to make your fear or your attachment go away, but simply to acknowledge your resistance as it comes up. By noticing your resistance, you don't identify with it.

Noticing the fear, you are not that fear. Noting your attachment to a specific outcome, you are not the attachment.

You don't have to indulge your desires or resist them. You just notice them and let them pass. As you hold each desire compassionately in awareness, it subsides.

Thoughts and feelings arise in consciousness and fade away. Nothing in particular makes them come or go. They are simply a diastole, like the rhythmic movement of the breath or the drum beat of the heart.

None of this means anything. It just is. It is the dance of being.

NOVEMBER 2

What If?

The ego-mind is always asking "What if?" It is forever exploring the possibility that there may be a better place to be, a better job, a better relationship, a better scenario than the one that confronts us here and now. All this is motivated by fear.

We don't experience what is directly, because we are too busy trying to improve it. Spontaneous acceptance of our lives as they unfold in the moment is quite rare.

November 3

Setting Limits and Respecting Them

Y ou can tell your friend what you want, but you do not have the right to ask her to change for your sake. The decision to change belongs with the other person.

If you really love someone, accept him as he is. Set the limits you need to set and give him space to make his own decisions. Be patient and do not pressure him to meet your expectations. Let him change because he wants to, not because you want him to.

Love your partner or friend as she is and allow her to be herself. Give her this freedom or you will lose your own.

There is nothing more difficult than trying to rescue or redeem another human being. It's like trying to save a drowning person with one arm tied behind your back. If you try to do this, you will either get pulled down and drown or you will escape feeling guilty for failing to fulfill a responsibility that never truly belonged to you.

Remember, it is a lot harder to undo a co-dependent relationship than it is to get into one. Better to stand back and empower the other person than to get drawn into a situation in which both of you betray yourselves.

November 4

Resting in the Center

mind is not the problem. It is how mind is used that helps or hinders.

When the reed is empty, blowing though it makes a beautiful sound, a sound that returns effortlessly to silence. When mind is still, thoughts arise spontaneously, offer themselves, and die in the wind. There is no complexity here.

The goal is not to make thinking go away, but to slow it down so that it comes to rest in its natural container. All that stands out about the individual, all that separates and divides, rests in that which has never known division. Call it love, compassion, heart-mind. Names do not matter.

Once you rest in that place, you no longer desire to be anywhere else. Once you rest in that peace, you cannot be attacked by your thoughts or anyone else's.

November 5

Prior to Thought

When thoughts cease, consciousness remains. When the breath ends, the reed still holds the potential of sound.

It does not matter if the reed is ever picked up. It does not matter if another thought arises on the screen of consciousness.

When thoughts arise, there is awareness of thoughts. When thoughts no longer arise, there is just awareness.

That which is prior to thought exists in you, but you can't find it by thinking about it.

november 6

Hide and Seek

ruth is ever-present. Our awareness of it may come or go, but truth remains as it is. Ironically, we become aware of truth when we relax and stop seeking it and we lose our awareness of truth when we start to look for it.

It is impossible for you to find your true Self because the part of you that looks for it is the very aspect that obscures it. As soon as truth is sought, it becomes hidden.

The great conceit of western esoterica is that truth can be found. This is the inevitable result of a mind out of touch with nature and its own physical embodiment.

Truth is. It can be experienced in the moment, but it cannot be conceptualized. It does not exist apart from the moment in which it is experienced.

november 7

Seeing the Lamp or the Lampshade

ruth is not exclusive. It belongs to all of us equally. Exclusive concepts of truth are delusional, no matter what tradition they come from.

All of us are beacons of light hiding under lampshades of different colors and size. And we always have the choice whether we will see the light in one another or be preoccupied with the lampshade.

Those who love you see the light within you. They don't focus on the shadows you cast.

november 8

Real Guides and Gurus

t he real guide or guru has no more of truth than you do. But s/he probably has less opinion, less prejudice, less narrowness, less need to argue, conceptualize, judge or condemn.

Having dissolved the barriers to truth for herself, the authentic teacher can help you recognize your own barriers. She cannot take you to truth, but she can show you how you stand in the way of realizing it.

november 9

The Potter and the Clay

y ou are one who decides what your life will be. You breathe life into every relationship and every circumstance which comes your way. Lest you gave it life, breath, meaning, purpose, it would have none. None of this exists apart from you. Yet you think it does.

The "you" you know is an effect, not a cause. This "you" identifies with outside things and defines itself in relationship to them. And so you are lifted up and dragged down, exalted and humiliated by all the myriad permutations of thought, emotion and experience. The "you" you know is affirmed by these identifications and injured by their perpetual rupture.

Why keep this drama going? Why seek stability and peace through that which is neither stable nor peaceful? You are not just the bowl or the cup, but the potter who turns it and shapes it. You are not just the clay, but the one who breathes life into it.

November 10

Feelings are the Door to the Heart

It's easy to read books and live our spirituality on the intellectual level . . . easy that is until life comes in and clobbers us. Then we are forced to go deeper in our spirituality.

We all want to feel peaceful, but life is not always peaceful. Sometimes difficult and challenging things happen and we need to get our arms around our entire experience. That means taking the time to courageously feel everything that we feel. Denying our feelings will not lead to peace.

People who are afraid to face their feelings can use meditation and other spiritual practices as tools for denial. They pretend to be happy when they are not happy. They try to get rid of their uncomfortable feelings instead of welcoming them as psychic messengers.

Our feelings are there for a reason. They are a pathway to the heart. Strong feelings come up when the door to our heart needs to open.

November 11

Completion

Don't be surprised when people come to you with the expectation that you make them whole. It is a common occurrence. But don't take the bait. You cannot complete another, nor can another complete you.

Each of you must find your own completeness. Each of you must know that you are already enough.

November 12

Turning the Other Cheek

When you see with your True Self you see only the True Self in others. To see with your True Self is to see beyond the masks that others wear to their essence. It is to see them through your love and acceptance of yourself.

When you see yourself with compassion, you see others that way, even when they try to attack you. You understand that they try to project their self-hatred onto you because it is too scary for them to look at it. So you don't attack back. You just remind them who you are and offer them the love they so desperately need and don't know how to ask for.

November 13

Taking Back what you Gave Away

You won't experience true intimacy if you spend your life trying to please others. You may seek approval and find it for a while, but it is only a matter of time before that approval becomes a prison.

One who gives herself away will have to take herself back sooner or later. One who looks to another for salvation will blame that other when salvation does not come. One who says "yes" because she is afraid to say "no" will say "no" in the end, but it will not be a gentle, compassionate "no." It will be the harsh, unforgiving "no" of one trying to survive, of one afraid of suffocating. It will be the cry of one who feels betrayed, although in truth she has betrayed herself.

November 14

Accepting Yourself

Y ou cannot "make" yourself love yourself, just as you cannot make yourself love others. Love begins with acceptance.

Practice acceptance when you become aware that you are being critical of yourself and others. Just be aware and accept what is happening . . . don't beat yourself . . . and then hold your experience in a loving way. Tell yourself "I see that I am being critical and that means I'm scared."

Accepting yourself in each moment is spiritual work. It is an ongoing practice. Unfortunately, there are no shortcuts. God's love for you follows on your love and acceptance of yourself.

November 15

Learning the Lesson

O ften, you leave a relationship or break another commitment you have made because you don't want to deal with the fears that are coming up for you. This exit strategy never works, because you will just turn around and create another relationship or another situation in which the same fears need to be faced.

You cannot leave your lesson before you learn it. You may need to experience that lesson with twenty different people in twenty different ways, but in the end you have to face your fears.

november 16

Bringing Love to Yourself

Your spiritual work is with your fears, not with anyone else's. Being aware of your fears clears out a space for others to become present with you. This never fails.

The ego tries to love, but it cannot do it. It knows only how to demand. Love does not come from the ego. But it must come to the ego, from you. Your love for the fearful part of yourself creates safety.

This kind of self-nurturing is the primary activity of spiritual life. When you bring love to yourself, ego is not a problem. It's only a problem when you are not bringing love.

november 17

Needing to be Liked

It is not necessary that other people like you. It's nice when they do, but it should not be devastating when they don't.

Self-worth must be established independently of the thoughts and feelings of other people. Then it is authentic. It is substantial. It is a reservoir of emotional strength that can be drawn on in times of emotional need.

novemBeR 18

Justice and Injustice

J ustice, fairness, and equality are often elusive. We don't come into this world with the same amount of talent or resources. Our good deeds are not necessarily rewarded nor are our mistakes always corrected in this life.

If there is a kind of spiritual justice, it is not a linear proposition. Some of the kindest and most generous people still get cancer and die and some of the most violent and abusive people get away seemingly without consequences.

God doesn't have a police force or even a hit squad, so if you are looking for some kind of causal or symmetrical justice, you may be disappointed. But if you look at things in the long haul, you see that our thinking and the actions that arise from them eventually catch up to us. A wolf just isn't happy wearing sheep's clothes forever.

Whatever is in the mind will eventually come out. It can't be hidden indefinitely. In the end, the chickens come home to roost. The unseen becomes visible. Sin can no longer be disguised by the elaborate robes of money, power, privilege or authority.

NOVEMBER 19

Seeking Love

The love seeker and the love giver live in different worlds. The love seeker doesn't know how to love. She is so concerned with how much she is getting, she doesn't have time to give to others. Forever counting and measuring, she goes into her head and closes down her heart.

Yet until she offers love, she will be miserable. Until she gives without expectation of return, the love that comes back to her will never seem to be enough.

NOVEMBER 20

Needing to Be Right

Our need to be right is an admission of egocentricity and self-righteousness. One who needs to be right rarely is, and when he is, it is at great price to himself and others.

Conceit and intellectual pride stand in the way of our awakening. They short circuit our learning process. When we are hung up on what we know, we forget that we don't know very much at all. We begin to take ourselves far too seriously. And that means that we have fewer friends and less peace of mind.

If we want to live in a more peaceful way, we must recognize our need to be right as a sign of intellectual immaturity and emotional weakness. It does not serve our need to grow or to be nourished in our relationships with others.

NOVEMBER 21

Finding your Calling

Finding a job and finding your gift are not the same process. Anyone can get a job. Very few people find their gift.

The Source of your gift is not outward, but inward. You will not find it if you are looking for the approval of others. You must learn to give that validation to yourself.

You won't find it if you try to make the gift conform to the demands of the job. In the end, you may be forced to choose between one and the other.

Your gift is a calling. It is a lifework. It starts deep within you and it begins to externalize as you acknowledge it and trust it. It does not happen overnight.

The more you trust in your gift and give it without strings attached, the more it multiplies. You experience lack only when you don't trust your gift or when you place conditions on giving and receiving it.

NOVEMBER 22

Psychic Tremors

most of what we build in our lives will be reduced to ashes and dust. That is inevitable. What the mind creates must eventually be destroyed to make room for its new creations. All forms age and become obsolete. All buildings, no matter how painstakingly maintained, eventually decay. The basic structure becomes untenable and cannot be repaired.

Beliefs too are gradually undermined from within. In time, they become weak, porous, overly stressed and stretched. Some develop gaping holes which are obvious to others but a mystery to us. Yet when our house falls down around us, we are the ones who are most surprised. Our friends just shake their heads and say "we tried to tell you, but you wouldn't listen."

That shouldn't be so surprising. When you are spending all your time and energy trying to shore up your house, it's hard to believe that your efforts are in vain. Indeed, if you believed that, you would stop trying to fix things and just let them fall apart. You might even grab a sledge hammer and begin to help in the dismantling process!

Few of us are willing to grab the sledge hammer, even when it has become obvious that our cherished beliefs are not working anymore. We become attached to our own creations. And so the process of destruction happens unconsciously. Like an earthquake, it wells up from the depths of the psyche.

Change seems to come from the outside, but it happens with our soul's blessing. When our need for psychological change becomes great enough, the soul simply refuses to hold the old systems of denial in place any more and then the whole edifice comes crashing down.

november 23

Trust and Failure

When we fail, we think that we aren't good enough to realize our dreams. So we give in. We conform. We find a job or a relationship that offers us security.

Yet the truth is we didn't trust enough. We didn't have enough faith in ourselves or in others. We tried to control. We insisted on doing it our way. We got scared and moved out of the creative flow of life.

Life was not against us. We were not willing to trust life. We didn't like the direction the river was flowing in and decided to swim the other way. Then, we got tired and gave up.

We can blame the river. We can blame ourselves. Or we can see what we need to do and do it next time. We can trust the river and learn to swim with the current, instead of against it.

november 24

Peace in our Hearts

If we seek peace in form, we are usually disappointed, as most forms are easily broken. Only if we seek peace in our hearts can we find forgiveness for all the broken pieces of our experience.

november 25

Time to Heal and to Forgive

We are all a bit impatient with our own healing and atonement process. We want to forgive and undo our guilt right away. We get discouraged if we continue to feel angry, guilty, fearful or resentful months or years after these feelings first surfaced.

Unfortunately, or fortunately, depending on your perspective, we have to let our healing take as long as it takes! We can want to forgive, but we can't force ourselves to do so.

There are no shortcuts to atonement. However, we can learn to hold our fear or discomfort in a compassionate way. We can stop beating ourselves up for feeling guilty or not forgiving totally. When we stop putting so much pressure on ourselves to "be spiritual and do everything right," we can allow our healing to take place on its own timetable.

november 26

Less is Better than More

In the beginning we think "more" is the answer to our perception of not having enough. More money, more activity, more lovemaking. But, in time, we learn that "less" works better. Less stimulation, fewer relationships, less activity all lead to the deepening of our experience.

When we focus deeply on what happens, we assimilate it fully. Then, we feel satisfied. We know that we have had enough. We don't need more.

november 27

The Observer

most of our science looks at objects and events in the outside world. It rarely turns its lens on the observer. Einstein, being a playful man, discovered that the observer was the one variable not being looked at. When he began to look at the one who was looking, a new world was revealed.

And so the West discovered something the East had known for some time: "what you see depends on how you see it." In other words, there is no reality apart from the mind of the observer. Without consciousness, there is no experience.

If we want to understand the workings of the world, we can continue to study objects and how they behave. If we want to understand the nature of consciousness, we must turn our attention to the observer. The world of "inner space" is as vast as that of "outer space." Indeed, the secrets of one are likely to be found in the other.

november 28

Releasing Past and Future

Our greatest spiritual challenge is to be happy in this moment. We can't be happy if we are upset about something that happened in the past or worried about achieving some outcome in the future. We can be happy only when our energy is invested in working with what is happening here and now.

november 29

The Value of Experience

I f you knew the pain that would ensue when you ate the apple, you would not have eaten it. You had to eat the apple to know the pain.

That does not mean that the apple is bad. It doesn't even mean that the pain is bad. In a sense, both are necessary to the experience of knowing.

Real knowing comes from experience. That is why incarnation is necessary. You cannot know in a detached way. To know, you must become. You must experience.

Many people attempt to find spiritual understanding through conceptualization, but it never works. Thought can take you to the doorstep, but it cannot take you into the inner sanctum. If you wish to know what's on the other side of the door, you must open it and walk through.

november 30

The New Paradigm

I n new paradigm organizations, individuals act collaboratively. The contribution of each person is essential but no one is a star. The stars are retired as soon as the old paradigm begins to fades into oblivion.

In the new paradigm, people are valued for who they are, as well as for what they do. Hierarchies are replaced by Equalities.

december 1

Desire

While prayer, affirmations and other efforts to concentrate the mind sometimes yield results, they do so only when there is a strong desire behind the mental practice. Asking for something mentally is not enough. You must ask for it with your whole being.

That which you desire you bring forth. What you want most, you promote without hesitation, drawing resources to you, enlisting the support and enthusiasm of others.

All manifestation is based on desire. Without desire, there is minimal manifestation. When you try to bring forth what you want only halfheartedly, you succeed halfheartedly. But what you energetically and one-pointedly seek, overcoming all obstacles, comes to pass.

What you desire and think about most are the strongest seeds that you sow. Where you put your energy is where your life goes. Or, as Jesus said, "Where your heart is, there will your treasure also be."

december 2

Neither in Control nor Powerless

there are two ways that you can interfere with the spontaneous flow of abundance and grace in your life.
1. Think you can control what happens.
2. Think you are powerless to do anything.
Neither one of these beliefs is true. Both are extremes that lead to incorrect assumptions and dysfunctional behavior.

Of course, if you are a control addict, believing that you are powerless may bring back some balance. On the other hand, if you believe that you are powerless, a little empowerment might help.

We are neither powerless to change our lives nor able to control what happens to us. Instead, we are free to work creatively or reactively with the events circumstances that arise in our lives.

december 3

Asking for What you Want

When you know what you want, start asking for it. Don't demand it or beat people up with your expectations. Just ask for it directly. Tell people what you want in a polite, respectful way. And then give them the freedom and the space to respond to you honestly.

Do not put any pressure on anyone. But don't repress your desires just because you are afraid of how someone might respond to them.

December 4

Creating from the Perception of Lack

When we create out of the perception of lack, we create a lot of stuff that we don't really need. And then we have to find a way to get rid of it. It is time consuming, inefficient, and not good for the planet.

No matter how much stuff we make, we will never fill the hole in our hearts. The only way that hole gets filled is when we realize that we already have what we need. Then the "hole" becomes "whole."

If we knew that the love we seek was within us, we could learn to connect with it internally. Then we could bring love directly to ourselves when we felt incomplete or unworthy, and we could stop projecting our unworthiness outward upon each other and the planet.

December 5

True Rewards

Spiritual actions have significant rewards, but these rewards do not come to those who seek them. The gifts of Spirit must be offered with no ulterior motives or strings attached. They must be given for the benefit of others without thought of how they might benefit self

Gifts that are given spontaneously and in good faith return to the giver many times over. One who gives in this way lacks nothing of value and does not accumulate possessions that he does not need.

december 6

Love Doesn't Buy You More Toys

even if you decide to choose love right now, it doesn't mean that you will get a new Mercedes.

Choosing love is a more profound choice than the purveyors of crystals and the champions of abundance theory know, because it is not just the spiritual adult who must choose, but also the wounded child who isn't sure s/he is worthy of love.

If you believe the pundits of angel glitter, then you can click your heels right now and, like Dorothy, go right back home. Nobody can argue with you if it works.

But if it doesn't work, you might have to realize that Dorothy has a journey to make in the underworld. And there she will encounter both angels and demons. She will have to confront the darkness in order to find the light. Like us, she will have to come face to face with all the aspects of self and other that she dislikes, because that is what the journey to wholeness entails.

This isn't the cotton candy kind of love. It's not the instant oatmeal approach to salvation. It is the kind of love that takes a lifetime to learn to give and receive. It's the kind of atonement that happens in the trenches.

december 7

Grace

When we know that we are worthy of love, we no longer need to engage in a profusion of activities designed to prove our worthiness to ourselves or to others. Our inner sense of worth enables us to give love without demands or expectations, thereby creating the pathway through which love spontaneously returns to us.

Our relationship to the world, and therefore to each other, is no longer one of manipulation, struggle or greed, but one of trust in the natural unfolding of all organic processes. What needs to occur happens through us, because we are willing and able, not because our egos need it to happen to validate self.

Grace unfolds in our lives and we are naturally drawn toward events and circumstances to which we can contribute our energy and attention. Because we are flexible and cooperative, we meet our goals seemingly without effort.

december 8

A Foot Soldier for God

i magine if someone came to you and said "Here are my skills. Please use them however you want to address our mutual good. I absolutely trust you to remunerate me in a fair and respectful way." You'd hire that person in an instant, would you not?

When you are willing to contribute without being attached to the outcome, you are immediately enlisted in the work of Spirit. You become a foot soldier for God. You cease to serve your own limited perception of what is good for you and begin to serve the good of all.

december 9

Joining Together

a s individuals align with the law of grace in their own lives, relationships will take on a new meaning. What two or more individuals could not do alone will happen spontaneously as they join together. The creative synergy of such relationships will transcend individual needs and agendas, touching lives that never would have been touched otherwise.

December 10

The Two Faces of God

If you have a spiritual perspective, you cannot measure your success in life based on external factors. True success is measured by your ability to love yourself and others, not by the size of your wallet, the number of your degrees or the importance of your job description.

External factors change. If we are attached to them, we suffer when things shift. Look at what happened to Job. He lost everything that defined his life, except his faith. His faith enabled him to use every adversity as a means for going deeper into his love.

Sometimes, when we welcome God into our lives, S/he decides to clean house and for a while our whole life seems a shambles. Job isn't the only one who found that out. You may be finding it out too.

God is both Vishnu, the preserver, and Shiva, the destroyer. With one hand S/he destroys our illusions and with the other S/he helps us develop our love and compassion.

december 11

Guidance

Guidance comes when you are feeling relaxed and peaceful. Gradually, you learn to trust the wisdom that comes to you in this relaxed, peaceful state, to speak the words you are guided to say, and to take the actions you are inwardly directed to take, even if you don't fully understand why you are being asked to take them.

Intuitive knowledge is based on "feeling right" about what you say and do, and not on coming up with an analytical solution. Later, as your look back on what happens, you may see why you were guided to speak or act in a particular way.

Often, the most accurate guidance you receive will be completely unexpected. That is because it comes from a deep level of psychic integration in which all aspects of consciousness are patiently accepted. This is the level of unity consciousness and solutions that come from this place often seem peculiar to the ego mind that is looking at the problem or dilemma.

december 12

The Spirit of the Law

a system of external laws can never provide the specific guidance we need to live our lives in alignment with Spirit. In order to live in alignment, we must learn to hear the voice of truth within our own hearts.

The law is not static. While it may come from a great spiritual Source, it must be expressed in a specific language and in terms that can be understood by people with a certain culture and experience. What speaks to one people at one time in history may or may not speak to another people at another time in history.

Rigid applications of the law are neither insightful nor compassionate. Instead, the inner meaning of the law must be divined so that it can be applied to the unique circumstances of the individual.

december 13

A Block to Learning

the greatest of all illusions is to pretend that you know something that you don't know.

Genuine ignorance is never a problem. When you don't know, you can learn. You are teachable. But when you don't know and think that you do know, you are not teachable. You have established a block to learning. This is worse than ignorance. It is outright self-deception!

december 14

The Wheel of Karma

internal states obviously have an impact on actions and actions have an impact on internal states. What happens outside and what happens inside are connected, not in a straight line, but in a circular way.

We all tend to give back what we receive and to receive what we have given. To get off the wheel of Karma, we must make a rare and courageous choice: to give back something different than we have received or to receive something different than we have given. Jesus underscored that when he asked us to love our enemies.

Of course, loving our enemies doesn't mean that they will choose to love us. It just means that we offer them an opportunity to choose love. Whether they do or not is up to them.

december 15

The Open Door

those who knock on the door will find it opened to them. Those who stand at the door too proud to knock will not be heard, but that is their choice.

God does not withhold love or truth from anyone. But only those who have open hearts and minds will receive these gifts.

Our job is to remove the barriers we have erected to love and truth. When our hearts and minds are open, all the gifts of God can be entrusted to us.

december 16

Challenging Untruth

When Jesus encountered an untruth, he challenged it. For forty days in the desert he challenged every fear-based thought that came into his mind. If you were willing to do this for forty days, you might wake up too!

Lies must be challenged where they are: in consciousness. It is not enough just to challenge the lies that are spoken. You must challenge the unspoken lies as well.

This is an important spiritual practice: challenge every unloving thought you have about yourself or other people. As long as these thoughts go unchallenged, you will feel separate from your true Self and the true Self of others.

december 17

How You Address Others

Realize that it is not what you do or what you say that is most important. It is how you act and how you talk to people. Don't address others when you are upset. Wait until you are feeling more peaceful. Only when you can speak the truth in a loving way can others can hear what you have to say without feeling attacked.

december 18

Inner Listening

many people say all the right words, but they have no understanding. They are just repeating what others have said. They are reading from a book. They are not in communion with their own experience, which is the only place genuine wisdom can be found.

That is why Jesus and other great teachers ask us not just to study what the tablets and commentaries say, but to be present in our lives in such a way that we are always listening for the direction of Spirit. They ask us to cultivate a direct relationship with God.

They are talking about process, not outcome. They are inviting us into a process of inner listening in which the truth can be heard and acted on. They do not tell us what that truth is in advance, because they want us to discover it in the moment.

december 19

Two Commandments

J esus knew that some of us would have trouble remember-
ing all ten commandments, so he decided to simplify the
teaching for us. He gave us just two commandments to
remember: "Love God with all your heart and mind and love
your neighbor as yourself."

To love God, we must realize that God is not only outside
us, but within us. S/He is in our heart and our mind. S/He is
intimate with us. Indeed, God's love and presence are the very
essence of what we are. To love God means to love and honor
ourselves, and to listen to and act on our guidance.

Yet just as God is our essence, S/He is also the essence of each
one of our brothers and sisters. And each of our neighbors
deserves the self-same honor, love and respect that we do. To
love God also means to love and honor our brother and sister,
and to respect their guidance and the actions that flow from it.

We cannot love God and dishonor ourselves or our neighbor. Loving God is intimately connected with our love for
ourselves and our love for other people.

december 20

Roots and Branches

i f you are a romantic, you will tend to have tragic relationships. Romantics have such high expectations of each other, they can't possibly live up to them. If you are a pessimist, you will tend to have uninspiring relationships. Pessimists have minimal expectations of each other and meet them without challenge. While romantics are bouncing in and out of relationships with great melodrama, pessimists are growing gargantuan roots in relationships that lack energy and intimacy.

You do not have to choose between a relationship that has wings but no stability and a relationship that has roots but no wings. Either choice is limiting.

Instead, be aware of your tendency and try to balance it. If your roots are massive, send some energy into the branches. Reach out and take some risks. If you are overextended and out on a limb, send some energy back into the earth and get grounded.

december 21

Not Knowing

oday is a day of rest, a day of meditation, a day of going inward. It is a day to surrender the past, to forgive, to let go of the aspects of your life that no longer work. It is a day to affirm the essence of who you are and to open yourself to a new vision of the future.

It is not a day for action or analysis. It is not a day when you can figure anything out or get any kind of external work done. It is a day to be quiet and to commune with yourself.

If you receive this date in divination, it will not be helpful for you to seek an answer to your question at this time. You will find the answer when you stop looking for it. So relax and take a few deep breaths. Go for a long walk. Just breathe and be and trust your inner wisdom to unfold.

Reading books is not spiritual work per say. They help us understand what the scope of the journey is, but they don't walk it for us.

Paul Ferrini's unique blend of radical Christianity and other wisdom traditions goes beyond self-help and recovery into the heart of healing. His conferences, retreats, and *Affinity Group Process* have helped thousands of people deepen their practice of forgiveness and open their hearts to the divine presence in themselves and others.

For more information on Paul's workshops, retreats, or *Affinity Group Process,* visit our web-site at ***www.paulferrini.com.*** You can send email to **heartway@crocker.com** or write to **Heartways Press, P. O. Box 99, Greenfield, MA 01302.**

New Releases from Heartways Press

The Companion Card Deck to this book!
Order this deck and transform this Book of Days
into a Spiritual Oracle.

Wisdom Cards: Spiritual
Guidance
for Every Day of our Lives
ISBN 1-879159-50-3 $10.95

Each full color card features a beautiful
painting evoking an archetypal theme.

Wisdom Cards will help you open to the
source of wisdom within your own consciousness and determine
propitious times for a significant event or project. These cards can
be used in conjunction with the book *Everyday Wisdom* or independently of the book. An instruction booklet is included.

A Classic work certain to become required reading in all Divinity Schools

Forbidden Fruit: Unraveling the Mysteries of Sin, Guilt and Atonement
by Paul Ferrini
ISBN 1-879159-48-1
160 pages paperback $12.95

Adam and Eve were not just naughty, disobedient children. They were created in God's image. They had God's desire for creative expression and awareness. As long as they remained in the Garden, they could not take the next step in their evolution.

How do you convince a dependent, obedient child to leave home, especially if there is a comfortable bed and three gourmet meals served every day? Adam and Eve weren't going to make a conscious choice to leave the comforts of the Garden. The choice had to be made at an unconscious level. They were driven by a desire they did not yet understand.

And so these two archetypal beings began a spiritual journey that would take them from sin to atonement, from ignorance to knowledge, from denial to responsibility. They would have to explore their darkness to find the light. They would have to become sinners to discover the blueprint for their redemption. They would have to experience the limits of their bodies, their minds and the three dimensional world to know that their true nature transcended all this. To become God, they had to first become human.

The Living Christ: Conversations with a Teacher of Love
by Paul Ferrini
ISBN 1-879159-49-X
256 pages paperback $14.95

Paul: Is it true that you are the Christ?

Jesus: Yes, and so are you and everyone else who learns to love and accept self and others. If you practice what I came to teach, you will begin to realize that the Christ nature is the essence of each person . . . Christ is the light born in the darkness. It is the flame of self acceptance that extends to others and eventually to all. He is rebirth of love in a world driven by fear.

Dancing with the Beloved: Opening our Hearts to the Lessons of Love
by Paul Ferrini
ISBN 1-879159-47-3
160 pages paperback $12.95

Romance may open the door to love, but it does not help us walk through it. Something else is needed. Something deeper. Something ultimately more real. . . . Challenging times must be weathered. Love must be strengthened beyond neediness and self-interest. It must die a thousand deaths to learn to rise like the phoenix beyond adversity of any kind.

Love is not a fragile, shiny thing, kept separate from the pain and misery of life. It is born of our willingness to learn from our mistakes and encounter the depth of our pain, as well as our partner's pain.

Enlightenment for Everyone
by Paul Ferrini
with an Introduction by Iyanla Vanzant
ISBN 1-879159-45-7
160 pages hardcover $16.00

Enlightenment is not contingent on finding the right teacher or having some kind of peak spiritual experience. There's nothing that you need to get, find or acquire to be enlightened. You don't need a priest or rabbi to intercede with God for you. You don't need to memorize scripture or engage in esoteric breathing practices. You simply need to discover who you already are and be it fully. This essential guide to self-realization contains eighteen spiritual practices that will enable you to awaken to the truth of your being.

The Great Way of All Beings:
Renderings of Lao Tzu
by Paul Ferrini
ISBN 1-879159-46-5
320 pages hardcover $23.00

Paul Ferrini's luminous new translation captures the essence of Lao Tzu and the fundamental aspects of Taoism in a way that no single book ever has! Part one, *River of Light*, is an intuitive, spontaneous rendering of the material that captures the spirit of the *Tao Te Ching*, Part Two is a more conservative translation of the *Tao Te Ching* that attempts as much as possible to stay with the words and images used in the original text.

Reflections of the Christ Mind Series

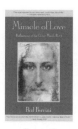

Part 1   Part 2   Part 3   Part 4

The four books in the *Christ Mind* series have changed the lives of hundreds of thousands of readers, bringing both believers and unbelievers alike face to face with the greatest teacher of our time. Here at last is a gospel devoted solely to Jesus' teachings of love, healing, and forgiveness. The teacher we meet in these pages is both compassionate and open-minded—he is the Jesus we know in our hearts. Repudiating religious hypocrisy, intolerance, and spiritual pride, he rejects the dogmatic position of the Church, offering instead words of hope and healing that form the new gospel for today.

Part One: Love Without Conditions
200 pages ISBN 1-879159-15-5 $12.00

Part Two: The Silence of the Heart
286 pages ISBN 1-879159-16-3 $14.95

Part Three: Miracle of Love
200 pages ISBN 1-879159-23-6 $12.95

Part Four: Return to the Garden
200 pages ISBN 1-879159-35-x $12.95

Selections from the Christ Mind Material

I am the Door

In this lovely lyrical collection, we hear the voice of Jesus speaking directly to us about practical topics of everyday life like work and livelihood, relationships, community, forgiveness, spiritual practices, and miracles. A beautiful introduction to the Christ Mind teachings.

288 pages Hardcover   ISBN 1-879159-41-4 $21.95

The Way of Peace
A New System of Spiritual Guidance

Drawing from the *Christ Mind* teachings, *The Way of Peace* empowers you to connect with peace within and act in harmony with your true self and the unique circumstances of your life. Like the *I-Ching* and *The Book of Runes,* this book is designed to be used as an oracle. It can be ordered with special dice blessed by the author,

256 pages Hardcover   ISBN 1-879159-42-2 $19.95

Reflections of the Christ Mind:
The Present Day Teachings of Jesus
Introduction by Neale Donald Walsch

A comprehensive selection representing the most important teachings in the *Christ Mind* series, published by Doubleday.

302 pages Hardcover ISBN 0-385-49952-3 $19.95

Two Best-selling
Relationship Books

The relationship book you've been waiting for

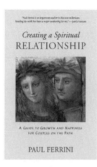

PAUL FERRINI

Creating a Spiritual Relationship

This simple but profound guide to growth and happiness for couples will help you and your partner weather the ups and downs of your relationship so that you can grow together and deepen the intimacy between you.

128 pages Paperback
ISBN 1-879159-39-2 $10.95

A practical manual for moving from fear to love

The Twelve Steps of Forgiveness

This book gives us a step-by-step process for moving through our fears, projections, judgments, and guilt so that we can take responsibility for creating the life we want. With great gentleness, we learn to embrace our lessons and to find equality with others.

144 pages Paperback ISBN 1-879159-10-4 $10.00

Two Practical Manuals
for Transforming Self and Society

Living in the Heart:
The Affinity Process and the
Path of Unconditional Love and
Acceptance

The definitive book on the Affinity Process! Now, you can learn how to hold a safe, loving, non-judgmental space for yourself and others which will enable you to open your heart and move through your fears.

If you are a serious student of the Christ Mind teachings, this book is essential for you. It will enable you to begin a spiritual practice which will transform your life and the lives of others. It will also offer you a way of extending the teachings of love and forgiveness throughout your community.

128 pages Paperback ISBN 1-879159-36-8 $10.95

Taking Back Our Schools

Based on Paul's experience home-schooling his daughter, this book is written for parents who are concerned about the education of their children. It presents a simple idea that could completely transform the educational system in this country.

128 pages Paperback ISBN 1-879159-43-0 $10.95

Wisdom Books

Illuminations on the Road to Nowhere

There comes a time for all of us when the outer destinations no longer satisfy and we finally understand that the love and happiness we seek cannot be found outside of us. It must be found in our own hearts, on the other side of our pain.

This provocative book challenges many of our basic assumptions about personal happiness and the meaning of our relationship with others and with God.

160 pages   Paperback   ISBN 1-879159-44-9 $12.95

Grace Unfolding: The Art of Living A Surrendered Life

This book is not about surrender to an outside authority, but to an inside one. It is about the relinquishment of our ego consciousness, our separated states of heart and mind to a greater consciousness, to the essence of love which is the source of who we are.

96 pages   Paperback   ISBN 1-879159-37-6 $9.95

The Ecstatic Moment: A Practical Manual for Opening Your Heart and Staying in It.

A simple guide that helps us take appropriate responsibility for our experience and establish healthy boundaries with others. It contains many helpful exercises and meditations that teach us to stay centered, clear and open in heart and mind.

128 pages   Paperback   ISBN 1-879159-18-X $10.95

The Wisdom of the Self

Explores our authentic experience and our journey to wholeness. "The Self is not a bundle of actions or conditions, but an unconditional state of being. To know the Self is to allow everything, to embrace the totality of who we are, all that we think and feel, all of our fear, all of our love."

229 pages   Paperback   ISBN 1-879159-14-7 $12.00

The Body of Truth

A crystal clear introduction to the universal teachings of love and forgiveness. This book traces all forms of suffering to negative attitudes and false beliefs, which we have the ability to transform.

64 pages   Paperback
ISBN 1-879159-02-3 $7.50

Forgiveness & Inner Child Books

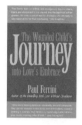

The Wounded Child's Journey
Into Love's Embrace

This book explores a healing process in which we confront our deep-seated guilt and fear, bringing love and forgiveness to the wounded child within. By surrendering our judgments of self and others, we overcome feelings of separation and dismantle co-dependent patterns that restrict our self-expression and ability to give and receive love.

225 pages Paperback SBN 1-879159-06-6 $12.00

The Bridge to Reality

A Heart-Centered Approach to *A Course in Miracles* and the process of inner healing. Sharing his experiences of spiritual awakening, Paul emphasizes self-acceptance and forgiveness as cornerstones of spiritual practice. Presented with beautiful photos, this book conveys the essence of *The Course* as it is lived in daily life.

192 pages Paperback ISBN 1-879159-03-1 $12.00

From Ego to Self

108 illustrated aphorisms designed to offer you a new way of viewing conflict situations so that you can overcome negative thinking and bring more energy, faith and optimism into your life.

144 pages Paperback ISBN 1-879159-01-5 $10.00

everday wisdom

Meditation/Healing Tapes

The Circle of Healing

This gentle guided meditation opens the heart to love's presence and extends that love to all the beings in your experience. This tape is designed to help you experience energy in all of your chakras and to feel the ecstasy of God-communion.

ISBN 1-879159-08-2 $10.00

Healing the Wounded Child

A potent healing tape that accesses old feelings of pain, fragmentation, self-judgment and separation and brings them into the light of conscious awareness and acceptance. Side two includes a hauntingly beautiful "inner child" reading from The Bridge to Reality.

ISBN 1-879159-11-2 $10.00

Forgiveness: Returning to the Original Blessing

A self healing tape that helps us accept and learn from the mistakes we have made in the past. By letting go of our judgments and ending our ego-based search for perfection, we can bring our darkness to the light, dissolving anger, guilt, and shame.

ISBN 1-879159-12-0 $10.00

Books on Tape

Finally our Bestselling Title on Audio Tape read by the author

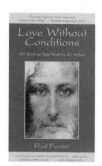

Love Without Conditions,
Reflections of the Christ Mind, Part I
The incredible book from Jesus calling us to awaken to our own Christhood. Approximately 3.25 hours

2 Cassettes ISBN 1-879159-24-4 $19.95

Poetry Books and Tapes

Crossing The Water:
Poems About Healing and
Forgiveness in Our Relationships
Our relationships help us heal childhood wounds, walk through our deepest fears, and cross over the water of our emotional pain. Just as the rocks in the river are "pounded and caressed to rounded stone," the rough edges of our personalities are worn smooth in the context of a committed relationship. If we can keep our hearts open, we can heal together and discover what it means to give and receive love without conditions.

96 pages Paperback ISBN 1-879159-25-2 $9.95

Available Light

Inspirational, passionate poems dealing with the work of inner integration, love and relationships, death and re-birth, loss and abundance, life purpose and the reality of spiritual vision.

128 pages Paperback ISBN 1-879159-05-8
$10.00

The Poetry of the Soul

Many people consider this cassette tape to be the most compelling of all of Paul Ferrini's work. These luminous poems read by the author are filled with wonderful nuances and insights. Come to this feast of the beloved with an open heart and open ears.

One cassette tape ISBN 1-879159-26-0
$10.00

Virtues of The Way

A lyrical work of contemporary scripture reminiscent of the *Tao Te Ching*. Beautifully illustrated, this inspirational book will help you cultivate the spiritual values required to fulfill your creative purpose and live in harmony with others.

64 pages Paperback ISBN 1-879159-04-X
$7.50

Talks and Workshop Tapes

Single Cassettes

Answering Our Own Call for Love
1 Cassette $10.00 ISBN 1-879159-33-4

The Ecstatic Moment
1 Cassette $10.00 ISBN 1-879159-27-3

Honoring Self and Other
1 Cassette $10.00 ISBN 1-879159-34-1

Seek First the Kingdom
1 Cassette $10.00 ISBN 1-879159-30-3

Double Cassette Tape Sets

Ending the Betrayal of the Self
2 Cassettes $16.95 ISBN 1-879159-28-7

Relationships: Changing Past Patterns
2 Cassettes $16.95 ISBN 1-879159-32-5

Relationship As a Spiritual Path
2 Cassettes $16.95 ISBN 1-879159-29-5

Opening to Christ Consciousness
2 Cassettes $16.95 ISBN 1-879159-31-7

Poster and Notecards

Risen Christ Posters & Notecards
11" x 17"
Poster suitable for framing
ISBN 1-879159-19-8 $10.00

Set of 8 Notecards
with Envelopes
ISBN 1-879159-20-1 $10.00

Ecstatic Moment Posters & Notecards
8.5" x 11"
Poster suitable for framing
ISBN 1-879159-21-X $5.00

Set of 8 Notecards
with Envelopes
ISBN 1-879159-22-8 $10.00

Heartways Press Order Form

Name _____

Address_____

City _____State _____Zip _____

Phone/Fax_____Email _____

Books by Paul Ferrini

Everyday Wisdom ($13.95)   _____

Wisdom Cards ($10.95)   _____

Forbidden Fruit ($12.95)   _____

The Living Christ ($14.95)   _____

Dancing with the Beloved ($12.95)   _____

The Great Way of All Beings: Hardcover ($23.00)   _____

Enlightenment for Everyone Hardcover ($16.00)   _____

Taking Back Our Schools ($10.95)   _____

The Way of Peace Hardcover ($19.95)   _____

   Way of Peace Dice ($3.00)   _____

Illuminations on the Road to Nowhere ($12.95)   _____

I am the Door Hardcover ($21.95)   _____

Reflections of the Christ Mind Hardcover ($19.95)   _____

Creating a Spiritual Relationship ($10.95)   _____

Grace Unfolding: Living a Surrendered Life ($9.95)   _____

Return to the Garden ($12.95)   _____

Living in the Heart ($10.95)   _____

Miracle of Love ($12.95)   _____

Crossing the Water ($9.95)   _____

The Ecstatic Moment ($10.95)   _____

The Silence of the Heart ($14.95)   _____

Love Without Conditions ($12.00)   _____

The Wisdom of the Self ($12.00)   _____

The Twelve Steps of Forgiveness ($10.00)   _____

The Circle of Atonement ($12.00)   _____

The Bridge to Reality ($12.00)   _____

From Ego to Self ($10.00)   _____

Virtues of the Way ($7.50)   _____

The Body of Truth ($7.50)   _____

Available Light ($10.00)   _____

Audio Tapes by Paul Ferrini

The Circle of Healing ($10.00)   _____

Healing the Wounded Child ($10.00)   _____

Forgiveness: The Original Blessing ($10.00)   _____

The Poetry of the Soul ($10.00)   _____

Seek First the Kingdom ($10.00)   _____

Answering Our Own Call for Love ($10.00)   _____

The Ecstatic Moment ($10.00)   _____

Honoring Self and Other ($10.00)   _____

Love Without Conditions ($19.95) 2 tapes   _____

Ending the Betrayal of the Self ($16.95) 2 tapes   _____

Relationships: Changing Past Patterns ($16.95) 2 tapes _____

Relationship As a Spiritual Path ($16.95) 2 tapes   _____

Opening to Christ Consciousness ($16.95) 2 tapes   _____

Posters and Notecards

Risen Christ Poster 11"x17" ($10.00)   _____

Ecstatic Moment Poster 8.5"x11" ($5.00)   _____

Risen Christ Notecards 8/pkg ($10.00)   _____

Ecstatic Moment Notecards 8/pkg ($10.00)   _____

Shipping

Priority Mail shipping for up to two items $3.95.   _____

Add $1.00 for each additional item   _____

Massachusetts residents please add 5% sales tax.   _____

Add an extra $2.00 for shipping to Canada/Mexico   _____

Add an extra $4.00 for shipping to Europe   _____

Add an extra $6.00 for shipping to other countries   _____

TOTAL   _____

Send Order To: Heartways Press P. O. Box 99,
Greenfield, MA 01302-0099   413-774-9474
Toll free: 1-888-HARTWAY (Orders only)
www.paulferrini.com
www.heartwayspress.com
email: heartway@crocker.com